Vegeta~~bl~~
medi~~c~~

Vegetables as medicine

Chang Chao-liang, Cao Qing-rong & Li Bao-zhen

A safe and cheap form of Traditional Chinese Food Therapy

translated by
Ron Edwards & Gong Zhi-mei

Pelanduk Publications
www.pelanduk.com

Published in 1999 by
Pelanduk Publications (M) Sdn. Bhd.,
(Co. No: 113307-W)
12 Jalan SS13/3E, Subang Jaya Industrial Estate,
47500 Subang Jaya, Selangor Darul Ehsan,
Malaysia.

Address all correspondence to:
Pelanduk Publications (M) Sdn. Bhd.,
P.O. Box 8265, 46785 Kelana Jaya,
Selangor Darul Ehsan, Malaysia.
e-mail: *mypp@tm.net.my*
visit us at: *www.pelanduk.com*

Perpustakaan Negara Malaysia   Cataloguing-in-Publication Data

Chang, Chao-liang
    Vegetables as medicine / Chang Chao-liang, Cao Qing-rong
    & Li Bao-zhen; translated by Ron Edwards and Zeng Ding-yi.
    ISBN 967-978-630-7
    1. Vegetables–Therapeutic use–China. 2. Materia medica,
    Vegetable–China. I. Cao, Qing-rong. II. Li, Bao-zhen.
    III. Edwards, Ron. IV. Zeng, Ding-yi. V. Title.
    615.32

Printed by
Potensi Serentak Sdn. Bhd.

FOREWORD

Vegetables are necessary to our diet. Not only do they contain abundant nourishment but are used to treat a variety of diseases. In China, treatment of diseases with vegetables has a long history, recorded in ancient Chinese medical and pharmacological books such as *Five Two Prescriptions*, unearthed from an ancient grave of the Han Dynasty in Mawangdui, Changsha. This is the oldest book of its type found in China in which the traditional medical use of vegetables has been recorded.

Liu Wangsu in the *Storage of Vital Energy in Familiar Conversation* (1188 AD), says, "Five kinds of cereals, five kinds of fruits, five kinds of domestic animals as well as five kinds of vegetables can furnish food and nourishment to supplement the vital energy and benefit the spleen and the stomach." In the *Compendium of Meteria Medica* (1578 AD) by Li Shizen, 1,892 kinds of medical materials were recorded. Among them 105 illustrated traditional medicinal use of vegetables, proving that the Chinese have effectively used them to prevent and treat a variety of diseases.

Vegetables are commonplace plants which can be easily recognised and obtained. An added advantage in using vegetables as medicine is that they do not bring about any side effects. Therefore, this form of treatment is not only simple and convenient but also effective and economical.

This book records more than 90 types of vegetables. These fall into the following groups: root vegetables, stem vegetables, flower vegetables, leaf vegetables, melons, fruits, beans, fragrant and acrid herbs and edible wild herbs. Descriptions of their appearances, nutritive value, flavours, attributive channel (indicating a relationship between medicine and channel), properties, applications, and precautions concerning the use of vegetables, plus clinical applications are extensively covered.

The authors wish to express their deepest appreciation to vice-chief physician Liu Ji-qun of the Guangxi Research Institute of Traditional Chinese Medicine and Pharmacology who read the manuscript of this book and contributed some additional information.

The Compilers, Nanning, China

A Note from the Translator

This book was written as a popular work for the rural population of Guangxi province and we have tried to keep it as comprehensive as possible, reducing medical terms to a minimum and using popular names for ailments rather than medical ones.

INTRODUCTION

This translation is a joint effort between myself and Zeng Ding-ji. My Chinese colleagues were supervised by the original authors and publisher and so we trust we have made it as accurate as possible.

For centuries the Chinese have relied on self-help for most minor ailments. In this way, a huge body of herbal lore has been absorbed into their culture. Over the years, these simple cures have been passed from one generation to another by word of mouth, but in recent years Chinese institutes of traditional medicine have begun to realise the value of this knowledge. As a result, researchers have been travelling to remote parts of the country, recording the various herbal treatments that are still in use.

Guangxi, in southern China, is very rich in this field due to two main factors. The first is that there is a large population known as the Minority People. These are mainly descendants of hill tribes who have retained not only their own languages but also a lot of their own culture, including their own herbal treatments. The second factor is that Guangxi still has a lot of mountainous country unsuitable for normal agriculture, and so is rich in other plants, including fruits and vegetables as well as wild herbs.

The definition of a vegetable as understood by the compilers of this book is a very loose one, and western readers may be surprised at some of the plants included here. However, rather than quibble over whether such and such a plant should be regarded as a vegetable, we should simply look on this extra information as a bonus.

In the west, market pressure is causing the variety of our vegetables to become smaller. China however, still retains a huge variety of vegetables, some of which are not generally known or used in the west. For this reason, not all the plants described in this book will be known to western readers. However, let us hope that in the future with an increase in trade and tourism between the west and China these less common vegetables will eventually find their way into our culture.

Caution: Great effort has been made to ensure the accuracy of this translation. However, the translators cannot be held responsible for the accuracy of the information contained. As mentioned, these are treatments used by ordinary people in China and should be regarded as such. If in doubt, or in the case of any major ailment, it is essential to seek medical help.

Ron Edwards

INDEX OF ENGLISH NAMES

CHINESE (Pinyin) INDEX

目 录

RADISH
Raphanus sativus L.
LUO BO

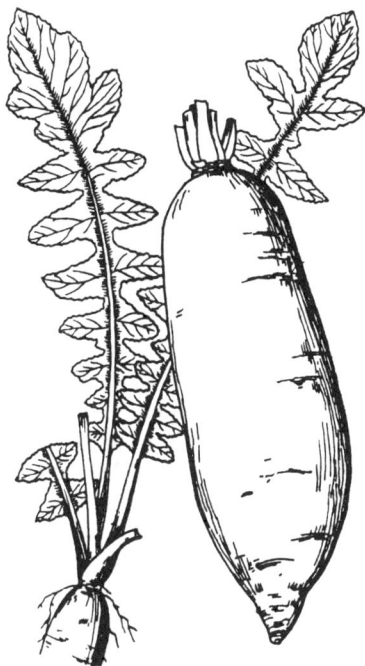

萝卜

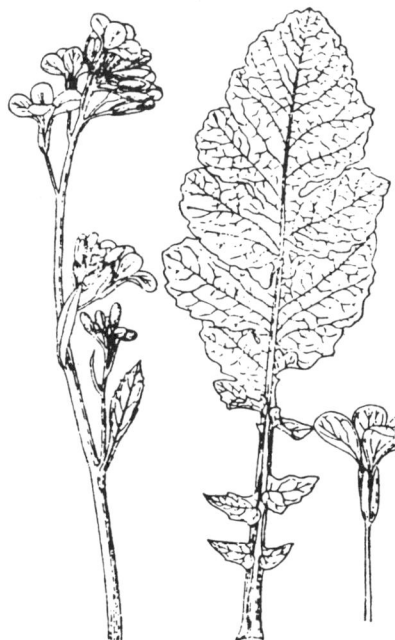

The radish, luo bo, is also called luo bai (plant white); lai fu (lamp quarter), lu fu (reed quarter) and tu su (earth-crisp). It is a root vegetable, usually an annual but sometimes living for two years.

The root is generally large but can vary in size and shape. Some are all white, others green on the top and white at the bottom, green on the outside and red inside, red outside and white inside, green outside and purple inside and so on.

The leaves are divided and have a feathery appearance. The seeds are egg shaped, small, flat and of a red brown colour. The leaves and seeds are used in medicine.

The root contains glucose, protein, calcium, phosphorus, iron, manganese, vitamins B1, B2, C, and radish glucoside. It is a good source of calcium. The seeds contain fat and oil. The leaf contains volatile oils.

The flavour of the root is bitter-sweet and its nature is cool. It is good for the lungs and stomach. The flavour of the leaf is slightly bitter and its nature is neither hot nor cold. It too is good for lungs and stomach.

The root can diminish sluggish feelings, clear feelings of heat and fever, disperse phlegm, keeps the qi (sometimes written as Chi or vital energy) from becoming over-active, warms the interior organs and helps neutralize poison. The leaf can diminish appetite and regulate the flow of vital energy. The seed can keep the qi from becoming over-active, help in the treatment of asthma, indigestion and clear phlegm.

APPLICATIONS
1. **HOT FEELING IN THE STOMACH WITH VOMITING:** Take some radish and cut it into

pieces. Add three slices of fresh ginger plus an appropriate measure of honey. Simmer and serve.

2. **HICCUPS:** Take some fresh radish and fresh ginger, crush together and obtain the juice, add a measure of honey then pour on hot water and drink.

3. **CONSTIPATION:** Slice about 500 grams of white radish, add a litre of water and simmer till it has reduced by half. Serve warm.

4. **WHOOPING COUGH:** Take 1.5 grams of dry white radish seed and grind to a powder. Add some sugar and warm water and serve three times a day.

5. **COUGH CAUSED BY WIND AND COLD:** Take a large radish plus some pepper and sugar. Dig a small hole in the top of the radish and insert the sugar and pepper. Bake the radish until the skin is golden and eat it warm. Do this every night before going to bed, for 3-5 days.

6. **DYSENTERY:** Take 100 grams of dried radish leaf, the older the better. Simmer in water to a thick liquid and drink as a tea. Do this frequently for 3-5 days. Alternatively take 50 grams of radish skin and 50 grams of purslane (a common garden weed). Simmer in water, then add honey and serve. If the dysentery has lasted a long time boil dried radish leaves with chicken meat and serve as a soup.

7. **HIGH BLOOD PRESSURE:** Obtain the juice from fresh radishes and drink a small cup of this twice a day for a week. Alternatively grind radish seeds to powder and serve 6 grams three times a day.

8. **BURNING FEELING IN THE LUNGS WITH COUGHING OF BLOOD OR BLEEDING NOSE:** Take an equal amount of the juice of the white radish and the juice of lotus roots, mix together and drink.

9. **COAL GAS POISONING WITH FAINTING:** Remove the patient into a place where the air is clean and circulating. Lay the patient down and pour small amounts of radish juice into their mouth until they wake up. Once awake the patient will feel nauseous and dizzy. Obtain fresh. radish juice, add some honey and let them drink this.

10. **POISONING FROM CASSAVA:** Take about 500 grams of radish, either fresh or dry, add an appropriate amount of brown sugar and serve.

WARNING: If suffering from asthenia (loss of strength) or cold feelings in the spleen do not eat this vegetable.

CARROT
Daucus carota L. var. sativa Hoffm.
HU LUO BO

The Chinese carrot, hu luo bo (foreign radish) is also called hong luo bo (red radish), hu lu fu (gourd turnip), ding xian luo bo (lilac radish), jin sun (golden bamboo shoot). It is a root vegetable, usually an annual but sometimes with a two year life.

The root is generally large but can vary in size and shape, long or short, cone-shaped, narrow and tapering or spheroid. In colour some are red, others yellow.

The leaves are divided and have a feathery appearance. The root (the carrot itself) is used in medicine. It contains protein, calcium, phosphorus, carotene, Vitamins B1, B2, anthocyanidin, fat, oil, volatile oil and a substance that can reduce blood sugar.

The carrot is sweet and its nature is neither hot nor cold. It is good for the lungs and spleen.

The root can strengthen the spleen, diminish sluggishness, help neutralize poison and assist in clearing a rash.

胡萝卜

APPLICATIONS
1. WHOOPING COUGH, (PERTUSSIS) IN SMALL CHILDREN. Take 120 grams of carrots and 12 Chinese red dates, add three bowls of water and simmer till they have reduced to one bowl. Serve this in several small portions in the course of a day and continue this for ten days or more.

2. MEASLES. Take 100 grams of carrot, 100 grams of coriander and 60 grams of water chestnuts. Add water and simmer till it has cooked to a soup. Take in small serves several times a day

3. CHICKEN-POX. Take 120 grams of carrots, 100 grams of coriander and 100 grams of chestnuts, simmer in water and drink as tea.

4. NIGHT BLINDNESS. Steam carrots and eat as part of a meal.

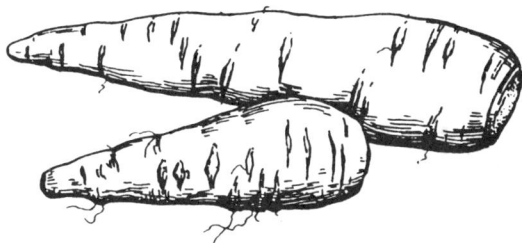

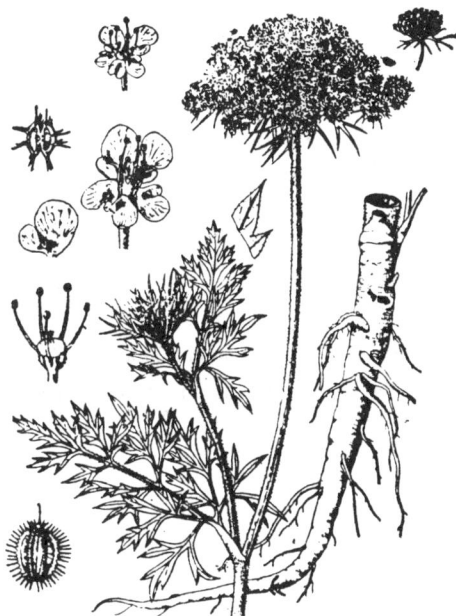

POTATO
Solanum tuberosum L.
MA LING SHU

The potato, ma ling shu (horse bell potato), is also called yang yu (foreign taro), tudou (earth bean), he lan shu (Holland potato); shan yao dou (hill medicine egg), shan yao dou (hill medicine bean) and de dan (earth egg).

The root is a stem tuber that grows in the earth, its shape is round or oval. Some varieties are all white on the outside, others are light red or violet. It is used in medicine.

马铃薯

Potatoes contain copious starch, Vitamin C and protein. They also contain a small amount of phosphorus, calcium, iron and fat and are highly nutritious.

The flavour of the potato is sweet, its nature neither hot nor cold. Raw potatoes are slightly cool in nature. They are good for the spleen and stomach.

Potatoes strengthen the spleen, acts as a tonic on the qi (chi or vital energy) and help neutralize poison.

APPLICATIONS

1. EMPTY COLD FEELING IN THE SPLEEN AND STOMACH; LOSS OF APPETITE; ANOREXIA. Take 100 grams of potatoes, 10 Chinese red dates, 6 grams of dried orange peel, and three slices of fresh ginger. Add water (and meat if desired) and simmer till the potatoes are thoroughly cooked. Season with salt and oil and serve.

2. HOT STOMACH PAINS WITH ACID REGURGITATION. Wash fresh potatoes, crush them and obtain a cup of the juice. Drink this every morning before breakfast.

3. MUMPS: Take a potato, wash it and then crush it with vinegar and obtain the juice. Smear the juice on the affected area. Let it dry and repeat at regular intervals.

4. BURNING AND SCALDING. Crush a potato to obtain the juice and apply to the affected parts.

WARNING. *If the potato is sprouting or has green patches do not eat this vegetable.*

SWEET POTATO
Ipomoea batatas (L.) Lam.
HONG SHU

The sweet potato, hong shu (red potato) is also known as shan yu (mountain tuber), fan shu (foreign potato), di gua (earth melon), gan shu (sweet potato), hong tiao (red trumpet-creeper) and bai shu (white potato). It is an annual. The tuber is plump and the shape may be round, oval or thick at one end. The colour varies according to the colour of the soil in which they have grown and the skin may be red, yellow or white. The flesh can be white, yellow, or pale mauve.

红薯

The stem generally lays flat, but there are some twining varieties. The leaf is usually egg shaped. The tuber and the leaf are both used in medicine.

The tuber contains abundant starch, carotene and vitamins B1 and B2 as well as quantities of protein, fat, phosphorous, calcium, iron, niacin etc.

The flavour of the tuber is sweet, its nature neutral when cooked or slightly cool when raw. It acts on the spleen and stomach. The flavour of the leaf and stem is sweet and insipid, its nature slightly cool. It acts on the lungs, large intestine and bladder.

The tuber can improve the flow of vital energy (the qi), promote secretion of saliva and moisten the stomach and intestines. The leaf can moisten the lungs and stomach, aid urinary problems and help clear pus.

APPLICATIONS
1. DRY INTESTINES, CONSTIPATION. Take a number of sweet potatoes and boil till cooked. Remove the skins, dip in honey and eat.

2. STOMACH ACHE: COLIC: VOMITING AND DIARROHEA. Take 100 grams of the vine of the sweet potato and cut into small pieces. Add a little salt and stir-fry until it begins to scorch. Add water and simmer till cooked. Serve one bowl.

3. STOMACH SWOLLEN AND PAINFUL; DRY RETCHING; CONSTIPATION. Take 250 grams of sweet potato vine and 6 grams of white alum. Simmer in water and divide into 2 or 3 doses and serve.

4. VOMITING BLOOD AND BLOOD IN THE STOOLS. Take 100 grams of sweet potato vine, simmer in water and serve. (Note, the vines can be dried and kept for up to three years.)

5. NIGHT BLINDNESS. Take 100 grams of sweet potato leaf, add pork liver, boil till cooked and eat. Serve 2-3 times in succession.

6. ULCER ON THE BREASTS OF NURSING MOTHERS; MASTITIS. Take the white heart of the sweet potato, wash clean, crush and spread on the breasts. Replace when the affected parts seem hot. Apply for a number of days.

7. SORES THAT BECOME INFLAMED OR POISONED. Take an appropriate quantity of fresh sweet potato and dandelions, wash, crush and spread on the affected place. This will help diminish the swelling and remove the poison.

8. HOT FEELING IN THE LUNGS WITH A COUGH. Take 250 grams of sweet potato leaf and 10 grams of ji xiang cao (lucky grass, *Reineckia carnea Kunth*), plus an appropriate measure of sugar. Simmer in water and serve.

CAUTION. Persons suffering from stomach pains, acid stomach, or half congealed stools should avoid this vegetable.

SWEET KUDZU VINE
Pueraria thomsonii Benth.
GAN GE

The sweet kudzu vine, gan ge, is also called ye ge (wild kudzu vine), fen ge (powder kudzu vine) and ge gen (kudzu vine root). The vine lives for several years. The root tuber is cylindrical and thick, the outer surface a greyish yellow and the inside powdery and full of fibre. The leaves grow in groups of three. Both tuber and flower are used in medicine.

The tuber contains a large quantity of starch as well as soybean glucoside, kudzu root yellow glucoside, amino acids, arachidic acid, etc. The flavour of the tuber is sweet but slightly pungent, its nature cool and it affects the spleen and stomach.

The flavour of the flower is sweet, its nature cool. It affects the stomach.

The root can help prevent muscles shrinking, promote secretion of saliva, prevent thirst,

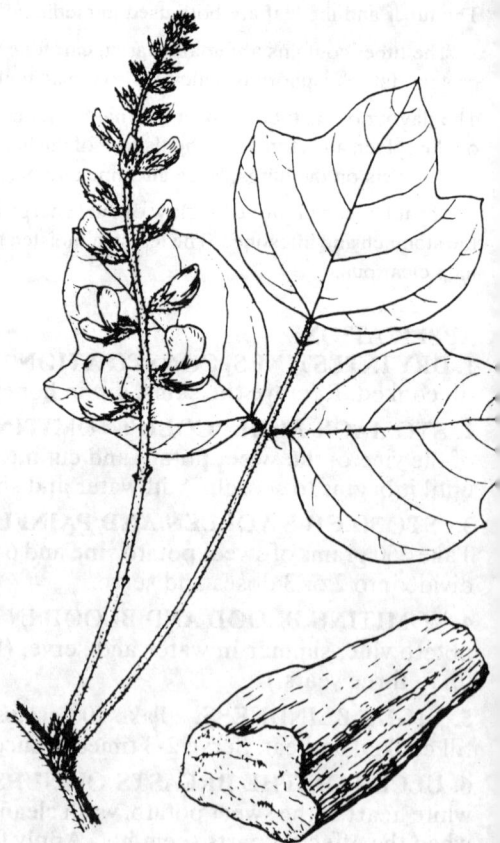

甘葛

16

clear a rash, help neutralize poison, remove adverse effects of alcohol, cool an inflamed stomach and stop diarrhoea. The flower can relieve the effects of alcohol and strengthen the spleen.

APPLICATIONS

1. FEVER WITH RESTLESSNESS AND THIRST. Take 250 grams of sweet kudzu tuber and 50 grams of millet grain. Soak the millet in water overnight, drain, add more water and boil with the kudzu vine till cooked.

Eat a small amount of this several times a day, warmed. It should cause sweating and aid recovery.

2. COMMON COLD WITH FEVER AND HEADACHE. Take 100 grams of sweet kudzu tuber, 10 grams of pale fermented soya beans and 7 spring onions. Simmer in water and serve hot. This should cause sweating and aid in recovery. When sweating has stopped eat a further serve.

3. VOMITING IN SMALL CHILDREN, WITH FEVER. Take 15 grams of sweet kudzu tuber and simmer in water till cooked. Add to rice soup and serve.

4. VOMITING BLOOD; BLEEDING NOSE; BLEEDING GUMS. Crush some sweet kudzu tubers to obtain the juice and drink this.

5. STOOLS HOT AND SHOWING BLOOD. Take an equal quantity of fresh sweet kudzu tuber and lotus root, crush together to obtain the juice and drink one cup.

6. SOBERING UP AFTER EXCESSIVE ALCOHOL. Take a quantity of sweet kudzu tubers and crush to obtain the juice. Slowly sip one rice bowl (or small soup bowl) of this.

7. HANGOVER; AGITATION; THIRST; TIGHT FEELING IN THE CHEST; VOMITING. Take 15 grams of sweet kudzu flowers, simmer in water and serve.

8. FOUL BREATH; RUN DOWN FEELING. Crush a quantity of sweet kudzu vine tubers to obtain the juice and drink one small cupful.

CAUTION. *If suffering from a cold feeling in the stomach with sweating avoid this vine.*

YAM BEAN

Pachyrhizus erosus (L.) Urban
LIANG SHU

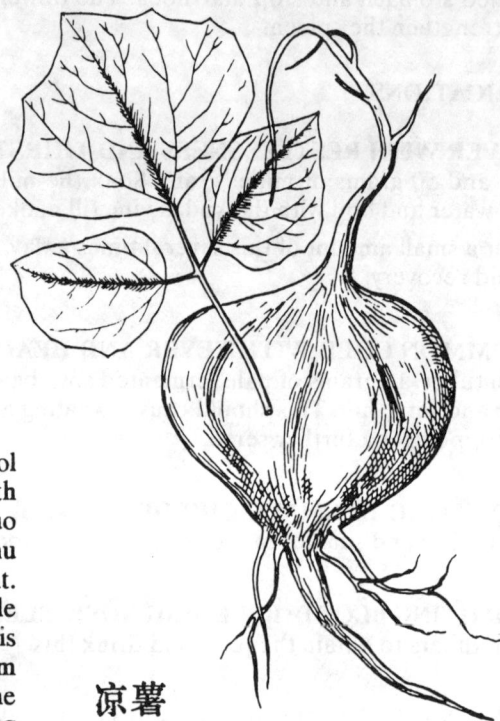

凉薯

The yam bean, liang shu (cool potato) is also called tu gua (earth melon) sha ge (sand kudzu), duo shu (bean potato) and ge shu (kudzu potato). It is a twining plant. The large tuber may be spindle shaped or like a flattened ball. It is fleshy and the outer skin cream coloured and composed of fine fibre. The flesh is white, containing abundant juice and the flavour sweet. The seed is yellow-brown in colour. Both tuber and seed are used in medicine.

The tuber contains starch and protein. Its flavour is sweet, its nature cool and it affects the stomach. The seed has a bitter flavour and its nature is warm. It is poisonous and has an effect on the lungs.

The tuber promotes secretion of saliva and stops thirst. The seed can kill parasites and helps cure scabies.

APPLICATIONS

1. CHRONIC ALCOHOLISM. Take a quantity of yam bean, peel and slice. Add an appropriate amount of sugar. Chew one or more pieces several times a day.

2. SCABIES. Take 30 grams of yam bean seeds and 10 grams of sulphur. Soak them in 200 mls of 75% proof spirit alcohol. After three days the mixture is ready to use and may be applied to the affected parts.

CAUTION. *If suffering from a cold feeling in the stomach avoid eating the yam bean. The seed is poisonous and should never be eaten.*

CHINESE YAM
CHINESE POTATO
Dioscorea opposita Thunb.
SHAN YAO

The Chinese yam, shan yao (mountain medicine) is also called shu yu (yam potato), shan yu (mountain potato) and huai shan (Huai Mountain). It is a perennial twining vine. The stem tuber grows vertically, is fleshy, cylindrical and can reach a length of 1.5 metres and with a width of 20-70mm.

The tuber is used in medicine. It contains mainly starch, but also has saponin, gum, allantoin, choline, arginine, amino acids, amylase, protein, fat, etc. Its flavour is sweet, its nature neither warm nor cool. It acts on the lungs, spleen and kidneys. It can rejuvenate the spleen, nourish the lungs, act as a tonic on the kidneys and improve sexual vigour.

山药

APPLICATIONS

1. LACK OF STRENGTH, RUN-DOWN WEAK FEELING. Take 30 grams of Chinese yam powder (shan yao fen), add water and boil till cooked. Add an appropriate amount of rice wine or sweet wine to make a paste like mixture. Take in the evening on an empty stomach. Frequent use should make the patient feel full of energy and bring a glow to the skin.

2. EXHAUSTION AND LACK OF STRENGTH; ASTHMA WITH EXCESS PHLEGM; SEMINAL EMISSION WHITE AND THICK; EXCESSIVE SWEATING; HEART PALPITATIONS; NERVOUS PALPITATIONS OF HAND, FOOT AND HEART WITH FEVERISH FEELING. Take 120 grams of Chinese yam, add water and boil to make 2 bowls full. Consume this much each day, taking frequent small amounts throughout the day.

3. FLOW OF URINE POOR OR TOO FREQUENT IN AGED PEOPLE. Take equal quantities of Chinese yam and white poria (*Poris Cocos*). Crush together into a powder. Twice a day take 15 grams, add water and boil to a paste like condition and serve.

4. ASTHMA; HOLLOW ASTHMATIC COUGH WITH EXCESSIVE PHLEGM. Take 30 grams of Chinese yam powder (shan yao fen) or 60 grams of crushed fresh Chinese yam. Add half a bowl of sugarcane juice (substitute raw sugar and water if necessary), simmer and serve hot.

5. LACK OF APPETITE; INDIGESTION. Take fresh Chinese yam and boil into a soup with water or Chinese yam powder (shan yao fen) boiled with water into a paste. Serve frequently.

6. DIABETES. Take 50 grams of Chinese yam, 15 grams of the root of *Trichosanthes Kirilowii*, 15 grams of *Adenophora stricta/latifolia* (ladybells), 10 grams of *Anemarrhena asphodeloides* (wind-weeds) and 6 grams of *Schisandra chinensis* (Chinese magnolia-vine). Simmer with water and serve.

7. SWELLING AT THE BACK OF THE NECK. Take a peeled Chinese yam and 2 seeds of castor oil plant. Crush together and apply to the affected place.

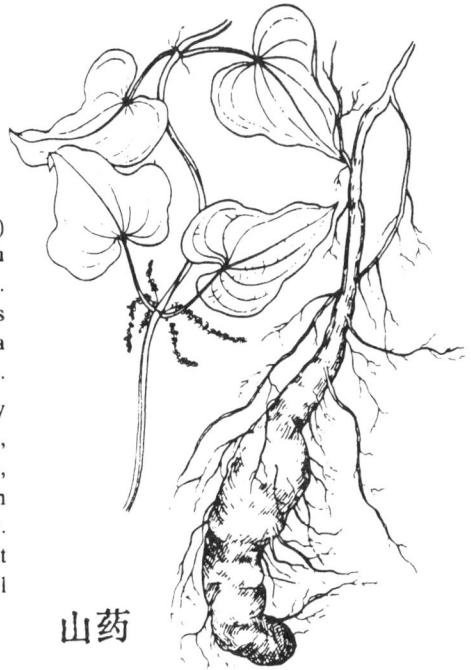

CHINESE ARTICHOKE
JAPANESE ARTICHOKE
Stachys sieboldii Miq.
GAN LU ZI

The Chinese artichoke, gan lu zi (sweet dew seed) is also called di can (cutworm), bao ta cai (treasure pagoda vegetable), di gu niu (earth bull), luo hau cai (arhat vegetable) and cao shi can (grass stone silkworm). A perennial plant growing 300- 1200mm.   The roots are horizontal and white, on the nodes grow a scale like leaf. At the end of the long roots is a tuber which may resemble a cluster of beads or a snail. The leaves are eggshaped or an elongated oval eggshape, with a leaf stalk that can reach 30mm. The flowers are pink or red-violet.

The tuber is used in medicine. It contains a large quantity of starch and sugar. Its flavour is sweet. Its nature neither warm nor cool and it acts on the lungs and spleen. It can improve the kidneys, moisten the lungs and nourish the blood.

甘露子

APPLICATIONS

1. HOLLOW COUGH; ASTHMA. Take 60 grams of Chinese artichoke, 10 grams of wood ear *(Auricularia auricula-judae)* and an appropriate amount of sugar. Simmer in water and serve.

2. KIDNEY AND WAIST PAIN. Take 60 grams of Chinese artichoke and 60 grams of black soybeans plus a pig's tail. Add salt and sesame oil to taste and boil into a soup until the beans are cooked. Serve a little several times a day.

3. PULMONARY TUBERCULOSIS WITH COUGHING BLOOD. Take 60 grams of Chinese artichoke and 30 grams of watermelon seeds (with the shells). Simmer in water and serve.

4. TUBERCULOSIS OF THE LYMPH GLAND. Take 60 grams of Chinese artichoke and 30 grams of tan hou cai (spit fire vegetable, see page112, *Murdannia braceata).* Simmer in water and serve.

5. A GENERAL TONIC TO BUILD UP THE STRENGTH. Take a fowl or a duck and simmer in water with a pig's trotter and pork bones, together with an appropriate amount of Chinese artichoke. This is highly nutritious and improves the physical condition of the body.

NOTES. *The Guangxi Chinese artichoke and the Northern Chinese artichoke are of the same family but different varieties. However their function and appearance are generally similar.*

CHINESE ONION
Allium chinense G. Don
XIE

The Chinese onion, xie, is also called jian tou (onion head) and qiao tou (buckwheat head). It is usually a perennial plant. The bulbs form in clusters and are egg shaped and about 10-15mm in diameter. The outer skin is white or pink and like a membrane, smooth without any cracks. 2-5 leaves grow from each bulb, cylindrical but showing 3-5 angles, the centre being hollow. The whole of the plant is used in medicine.

It contains garlic amino acids, methyl-garlic amino acid, garlic sugar etc. The flavour is pungent, its nature warm. It affects heart, liver and lungs.

It can warm internal organs and improve yang (of yin and yang), regulate the flow of vital energy, disperse poor blood and ease pain.

薤

APPLICATIONS

1. CORONARY HEART DISEASE; ANGINA PECTORIS. Take 15 grams of onion bulbs, 20 grams of Mongolian snakegourd fruit (*Fructus Trichosanthis*), 15mls of white wine and 200mls of water. Simmer until the mixture has reduced to 100ml. Take a small amount twice a day.

2. STOMACH NEUROSIS. (in traditional medicine called Ben tun gi, which translates roughly as "hurrying piglet's breath") Crush peeled onions to obtain one small cup of juice, and drink this.

3. COLD, WET DIARRHOEA IN SMALL CHILDREN, MOTIONS FROTHY AND FULL OF BUBBLES. Take 15 grams of the beard of the onion bulb, add water and simmer to make one bowl. Divide this into 3 serves over the course of a day.

4. SINUSITIS. Take 15 grams of peeled onions, 10 grams of pawpaw (papaya) flowers and 100 grams of pork snout. Simmer in water and serve.

5. MOVEMENT OF THE FOETUS ACCOMPANIED BY STOMACH PAIN DURING PREGNANCY. Take 10 grams of peeled onions and 10 grams of Chinese angelica (*Angelica sinensis*). Add water and simmer to obtain one bowl. Divide into two and take in the course of a day.

6. CHRONIC TRACHEITIS; BRONCHITIS. Take peeled onions and crush. 3 times a day take 3 grams of the juice and pulp with sugar and water.

7. ROUNDWORMS; BILLARY ASCARIASIS. Pickle the onion flower heads in vinegar for several days. Chew the heads or drink some of the vinegar.

8. STOMACH OR INTESTINAL INFLAMATION WITH DRY VOMITING; GASTROENTERITIS. Take 50 grams of onions and add 150 mls of water. Simmer till reduced to 100 mls and serve warm.

9. INADEQUATE ERUPTION OF MEASLES. Take onion leaves, dip in alcohol or wine and rub the affected parts.

10. SCABIES, ITCHING SORES. Crush fresh shallot leaves to obtain the juice and apply to the affected parts.

11. INSECT STINGS. Crush onions and apply the juice to the affected parts.

CAUTION. *Persons with diminished qi or lacking vital energy should be cautious in eating this vegetable.*

ONION
Allium Cepa L.
YANG CONG

The onion, yang cong (foreign onion) is also called yu cong (jade onion). The plant can live a number of years. The bulb is large and round or a slightly flattened ball shape. The outer skin may be red-violet, red-brown, pale reddish-brown, yellow or cream. The inside is thick and fleshy. The leaf is cylindrical with a hollow centre. The bulb is used in medicine.

洋葱

It contains cinnanic acid, caffeine acid, asafoetida acid, mustard seed acid, polysaccharide A and B, quercetin, many varieties of amino acids, calcium, phosphorus, iron, vitamin C, volatile oils, etc.

The flavour is sweet and pungent, its nature warm and it affects the liver and lungs. It can calm the liver and moisten the intestines.

APPLICATIONS
1. HIGH BLOOD PRESSURE. Take an onion, peel and clean it. Eat it raw or cooked.

2. CONSTIPATION. Take a clean peeled onion and eat it raw or stir fry it in peanut oil. Repeat for several days.

3. WOUNDS. Take an onion, clean it and crush, then apply to the affected parts.

4. ULCERS OF THE SKIN. Crush an onion and apply the juice to the affected parts.

5. VAGINAL TRICHOMONIASIS. Clean an onion and crush to obtain the juice. Use cotton wool to apply to the affected parts.

CAUTION: *Persons suffering from stomach problems should eat only a small quantity of onion.*

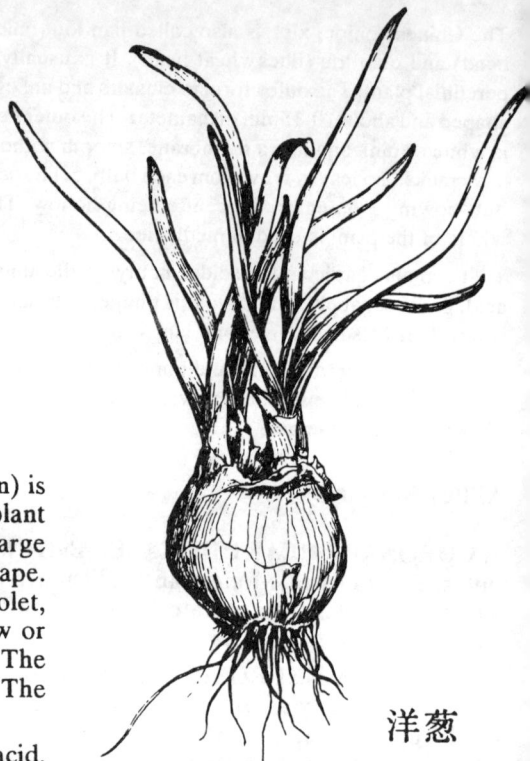

BAMBOO SHOOT
Bambusa beecheyana Munro
TIAN ZHU

The bamboo shoot, tian sun (sweet bamboo shoot) is also called diao si qiu zhu (hanging silk ball bamboo) and tian zhu sun (sweet bamboo shoot). A perennial plant, the stalk can grow to the height of a tree. The main stalk is curved and bent at the end in a young plant. The leaf sheath is 40-80mm long, the leaf 110-280mm long and 15-35mm wide.

The bamboo shoot is conical, the base 60-120mm wide, tapering to a point. The outer covering is in separate parts, rising from each joint, the outer face of it smooth or covered with very fine hair.

甜笋

The flesh is cream coloured, the flavour good, both sweet and crisp. The shoot is used in medicine. It contains auxin, docosanoic alcohol and unsaturated fatty acids.

Its flavour is sweet, its nature neither warm nor cool, and it affects the lungs. Bamboo shoots can control phlegm and ease some respiratory problems.

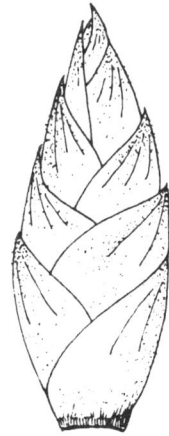

APPLICATIONS
1. SEARING COUGH WITH COPIOUS PHLEGM. Take 30 grams of bamboo shoots and an appropriate quantity of sugar. Simmer in water and serve

2. COMMON COLD. Take 30 grams of pickled bamboo shoots and an appropriate quantity of garlic, fermented soya beans and red peppers. Cook with noodles, adding a little salt and sesame oil for flavour. When eaten hot this should cause sweating, and to aid this the patient should be covered with a light quilt.

3. CHRONIC PROLAPSE OF THE ANUS. Take 500 grams of pickled bamboo shoot, and 100 grams of chicken flesh. Boil till the chicken is cooked and puree with a little salt for flavour. Eat a little 3 times a day and continue this for 3-5 days.

CAUTION: *People suffering injuries from falls, fractures, strains, liver illness, carbuncles or stomach problems should avoid bamboo shoots.*

WILD RICE STEM
Zizania caduciflora (Turcz. ex Trin.) Hand.-Mazz.
JIAO BAI

The wild rice stem, jiao bai, is also called gu (wild rice) and jiao sun (wild rice bamboo shoot). It is a hydrophyte, a perennial water plant. The stalk stands vertically.

If a fungus grows in the tender part of the stem it becomes swollen and is then called wild rice stem-melon. The parts of the stem not affected by fungus are called wild rice stem-vegetable. The leaf has a rolled needle appearance. The swollen part of the stem (jiao gua or wild rice stem-melon), the root, the fruit and the wild rice itself are all used in medicine.

The swollen part of the stem contains protein, fat, carbohydrate and phosphorous, as well as a small measure of calcium, iron, vitamins B1, B2 and carotene.

The flavour of the stem is sweet and astringent, its nature cool and it affects the liver and spleen. It can cool fever, calm fidgeting, alleviate thirst, promote lactation, and improve bowel and bladder motions.

The root calms fever and is an antidote for some poisons. The grain calms fever and nervous agitation, improves the flow of saliva and eases thirst.

茭白

APPLICATIONS
1. TO IMPROVE FLOW OF BREAST MILK. Take 30 grams of wild rice stalks and 10 grams of the pith of *Tetrapanax papyrifera* (stem pith of the rice-paper plant). Simmer with a pig's trotter till cooked and serve.

2. BURNS AND SCALDS. Take an appropriate quantity of wild rice root and bake to charcoal then crush. Mix with egg white and apply to the affected parts.

3. STOMACH PAINS CAUSED BY EXTREMELY HOT WEATHER. Take 30-50 grams of fresh wild rice roots, simmer in water and serve.

CAUTION: *If suffering from a cold feeling in stomach and spleen avoid eating any quantity of this plant.*

24

LOTUS ROOT
Nelumbo nucifera
OU

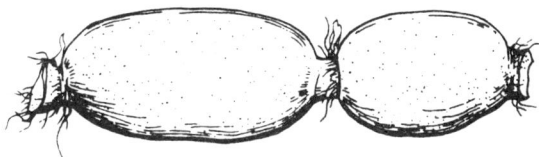

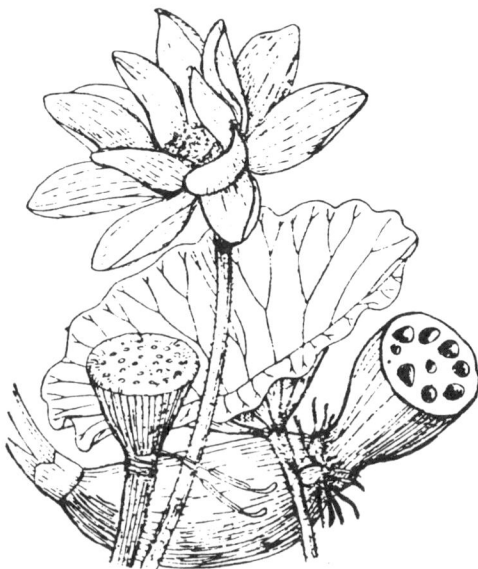

The lotus root, ou, is also called lian ou (lotus, lotus root), lian (lotus) and fu rong (cottonrose hibiscus). It is a perennial water plant. The rhizome grows horizontally, has a rough surface and is swollen between the joints. The inside is perforated with a number of holes running the length of the rhizome the size of which diminish towards the joints.

Both the rhizome and the joints are used in medicine. The rhizome contains starch, vitamin C, lucid asparagus element, albumen amino acids, trigoneline, lecithin, pentose, sucrose, glucose, protein, fat, etc.

The flavour of the raw root is astringent, its nature cool. When boiled the flavour is sweet, its nature slightly warm and it affects the heart, spleen and stomach.

The raw root can calm fever, cool the blood and clear blood poisoning. The boiled root improves the blood and invigorates spleen and stomach.

APPLICATIONS

1. DYSENTERY. Take 30 grams of lotus root powder and blend in some honey. Add water and boil to a paste to make one bowl full. Serve this twice a day.

2. CHILBLAINS; SPLITS IN THE FOOT CAUSED BY EXTREME COLD. Steam a lotus root till cooked, crush and apply to the affected place.

3. SINUSITUS: YELLOW DISCHARGE FROM THE NOSE. Take equal quantities of the joint of the lotus root and *Ligusticum wallichii* and grind together. Twice a day mix 5 grams in a bowl of rice soup and serve.

4. NOSE BLEEDING THAT WILL NOT STOP. Take 250 grams of fresh lotus root joints, wash clean and crush to obtain the juice. For each treatment take 20mls of this and also put some drops of the juice into the nose.

5. SUDDEN VOMITING OF BLOOD. Take 20 joints of lotus root and 7 pieces of the base of the lotus leaf, add water and simmer to make one bowl. Add a measure of honey and serve.

6. THROAT INFLAMATION. Take 10 joints of lotus root, simmer in water to make one bowl. Add a little salt and serve.

7. LUNGS INFLAMED AND COUGHING BLOOD. Take 30 grams of lotus root joints, 15 grams of *Rehmannia glutinosa*, 10 grams of madder charcoal, 10 grams of dissolved donkey hide gelatin, 10 grams of *Fritillaria thunbergii*, 10 grams of apricot kernel and 3 grams of licorice root. Simmer together with water and serve.

NOTES. *The leaf, stems, flower, stamen and seed are all used in medicine.*

KOHLRABI
Brassica caulorapa Pasq.

QIU JINIG GAN LAN

Kohlrabi, qiu jing gan lan, (corn sweet indigo), is also called jie lan tou (mustard indigo head) and bo lan (thumb indigo). The plant can live for two years and is short and robust, without hairs. The stem is short and swollen at ground level, ball shaped or like a flattened ball 50-100mm in diameter. The leaf is wide and egg shaped or oval, the edges saw toothed or irregular. The swollen stem is used in medicine. It contains protein, carbohydrates, calcium, phosphorous, iron, niacin, vitamins B1, B2, C.

球茎甘蓝

The flavour of the swollen stem is sweet, its nature neither warm nor cool and it affects the spleen and stomach. It can rejuvenate the spleen and diminish indigestion.

APPLICATIONS

1. **STOMACH ULCER; DUODENAL ULCER; INDIGESTION; LOSS OF APPETITE.** Take a quantity of kohlrabi, peel and slice and place in a glass or ceramic container. Add an appropriate quantity of honey and let it soak for two days until the kohlrabi becomes soft and the honey has soaked through. Take a piece as often as desired and chew it.

ARROWHEAD
Sagittaria trifolia L.
CI GU

慈姑

The arrowhead, ci gu (loving aunt) is also called ci gu (thatch wild rice). It is a perennial swamp plant. The rhizome is ball shaped or oval, the outer skin bare and smooth, in colour green or white and in size as large as a hen egg or a little smaller with a shoot on the end. The flesh is white, the flavour sweet and slightly astringent.

The green skinned corm is round, its flesh powdery, fragrant and thick, the flavour excellent. The white skinned corm is oval and large, the flesh coarse, the flavour astringent and bitter. The leaf has a distinctive 3 cornered arrow-like shape and is 50-250mm long. Both corm and stem are used in medicine.

The corm contains protein, fat, carbohydrate, calcium, phosphorous, iron, vitamin B, trypsin, etc. It affects lungs and heart. The flavour of the complete plant is insipid, its nature cool. The corm improves the lungs, stops coughing and bleeding and helps control the intestines. The complete plant calms fever, helps retain body fluids and helps neutralize poison.

APPLICATIONS

1. TUBERCULOSIS; COUGHING UP BLOOD. Take 60 grams of arrowhead corms, 30 grams of manna, 10 grams of *Auricularia* (wood ear fungus), and an appropriate quantity of sugar. Simmer in water and serve. Another treatment is to take a number of arrowhead corms, peel and crush, then add an appropriate quantity of honey and rice gruel. Mix together, steam till cooked and eat hot.

2. ASTRINGENT PAIN WHEN URINATING. Take 60 grams of the complete plant, simmer in water and serve.

3. YELLOW JAUNDICE. Take 60 grams of the whole plant, and 15 grams of day lily root. Simmer in water, sweeten with sugar and serve.

4. HEART PAINS AND BLOOD POISONING AFTER GIVING BIRTH. Take 60 grams of arrowhead corms, wash clean and crush to obtain juice. Drink this in one serve.

5. SWOLLEN AND PAINFUL BOILS AND CARBUNCLES. Take 60 grams of arowhead corms, wash clean and crush to obtain juice and serve this. Apply the sediment to the affected parts.

6. INSECT STINGS. Take an arrowhead corm, add a little salt and crush it. Apply to the affected place.

CAUTION. *Pregnant women and people suffering from constipation should avoid this plant.*

CHINESE CHIVES
Allium tuberosum Rottl. ex Spreng.
JIU CAI

Chinese Chives, jiu cai, are also called bian cai (flat vegetable), zhuang yang cao (robust male grass), qi yang cao (rising sun grass) and chang sheng jiu (long life chives). It is a perennial herb.

The bulbs form in clusters and are cylindrical. The outer skin is like a net and it has many roots. The leaf is a long strip, flat in cross section and not hollow. The flowers are white, the seeds black. Bulb, leaf and seeds are all used in medicine.

The leaf contains protein, fat, carbohydrate, calcium, phosphorous, vitamins B1, B2, C, and niacin. The leaf contains sulphide, etc. The flavour

韭菜

of the root is pungent, its nature warm, and it affects the liver. The flavour of the leaf is sweet-pungent, its nature warm and it affects the liver, stomach and kidneys. The flavour of the seed is salty and pungent, its nature warm and it affects the liver and kidneys.

The bulb can regulate the flow of vital energy and disperse blood poisoning. The leaf also helps regulate the flow of vital energy, disperses bad blood and helps neutralize poison. The seeds nourish liver and kidneys, strengthen the yang and helps stop nocturnal emission.

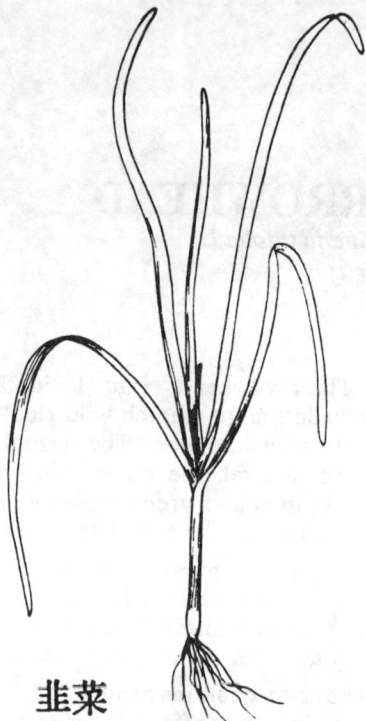

APPLICATIONS

1. FEELING OF WEAKNESS, SWEATING AT NIGHT; TUBERCULOSIS WITH SWEATING AT NIGHT. Take an appropriate quantity of chives and clam meat. Boil into a soup, add peanut oil and salt for flavour. A little rice wine or millet wine can be added when serving. Divide and serve 2-3 times a day.

Another treatment is to take 30 grams of bulbs, add 200 mls of water and simmer till reduced to 100 mls. Serve this at one time.

2. ACCIDENTAL SWALLOWING OF FRAGMENTS OF GLASS, METAL etc. Take 250 grams of chives, cut into small pieces 30-50mm long, boil till cooked, chew and swallow.

3. CHOKING FEELING IN THE DIAPHRAGM (seek medical help as this may be related to cancer of the oesophagus or stomach cancer, especially if there is difficulty in swallowing and constant vomiting after eating). Crush fresh chives to obtain the juice and sip very slowly. Another treatment is to add one spoonful of the juice to half a cup of milk and heat to boiling point. Sowly sip while it is still warm.

4. THIRSTY FEELING EVEN AFTER DRINKING; POLYDIPSIA. Every day take 25 grams of chives, stir fry and eat or boil with soup and eat. Do not add salt. Eat daily for 3 weeks.

5. IMPOTENCE; COLD PAIN IN THE WAIST AND KNEE; SPERMATORRHOEA, SEMINAL EMISSION.

(a) Crush some chive seeds and add to rice wine or sorghum wine in the proportion of one part of seeds to five of wine. Leave them to soak for one week. Three times a day take 10 mls of the wine after meals.

(b) Take 250 grams of chive leaves and 50 grams of walnut flesh, add a little sesame oil and stir fry till cooked. Eat this daily in one serve and continue the treatment for a month.

6. NOSE BLEEDING, EPISTAXIS; BLEEDING HAEMORRHOIDS; BLOOD IN THE STOOL; BLOOD IN THE URINE; IRREGULAR BLEEDING NOT ASSOCIATED WITH MENSTRUATION, METRORRHAGIA. Crush some chive bulbs to obtain the juice. Take 10-20 mls, mix with warm water and drink at regular intervals.

7. INDIGESTION WITH DIARRHOEA. Take an appropriate quantity of chives, stir fry and eat.

8. BECOMING DIZZY OR FAINTING AFTER GIVING BIRTH. Take a bundle of chives and a cup of vinegar. Chop the chives and place in a pot. Boil the vinegar and pour this onto the chives. Inhale the vapour.

9. VOMITING CLEAR LIQUID AFTER GIVING BIRTH. Take 500 grams of chives, wash clean and crush to obtain the juice, add some juice from crushed ginger and serve a little at a time.

10. ACHES AND PAINS AFTER FALLS AND TUMBLES. Take 250 grams of fresh chives, wash clean and crush to obtain the juice. Add hot water and sugar and serve.

11. SWELLINGS AFTER FALLS AND SIMILAR ACCIDENTS. Take 250 grams of chives, 100 grams of fresh ginger and 50 grams of onion. Crush together then add a little wine. Stir fry till cooked and while warm apply to the affected parts.

12. TINEA. Take 50 grams of fresh chives and 10 grams of borax *(sodium borate)*, crush together and apply to the affected parts.

13. NETTLE RASH, URTICARIA. Take an appropriate quantity of chives, add a little salt, crush and apply to the affected parts.

14. NERVOUS DERMATITIS. Take 250-500 grams of chives plus a litre of water that rice has been washed in. First take the rice water and put it to one side until it has turned sour. Drain off the clear liquid, add the rest to the chives and boil for 15 minutes. Allow to cool and wash the affected parts.

15. ALLERGIC DERMATITIS. Take some chives and hen feathers, simmer together and use the liquid to wash the affected parts.

16. SCLERODERMA IN BABIES. Take 60 grams of chives and 60 grams of rice wine. Take the chives, chop and stir fry till cooked. Add the rice wine and mix it in. Use a soft gauze cloth to swab the juice on the affected parts for 15-20 minutes at each application. Do this once a day and continue for 7 days as one treatment. The treatment can be used more than once if necessary.

CAUTION. *Persons suffering from a deficiency of yin, with high fever, or pregnant women should all avoid eating chives.*

AMARANTH

Amaranthus tricolor L.

XIAN CAI

(In the west the red variety is known as Love Lies Bleedin. The green variety is grown in some vegetable gardens but is not so well known. Ed)

The amaranth, xian cai, is also called qing xiang xian (green fragrant amaranth) and hong xian cai (red amaranth vegetable). It is an annual growing to a height of 800-1500mm. The stem is strong, without thorns. The leaf is egg shaped or pointed, 40-100mm long and 20-70mm wide, and may be green, red, purple or yellow. The flowers form a spike at the top of the plant and hang down, often in a cluster.

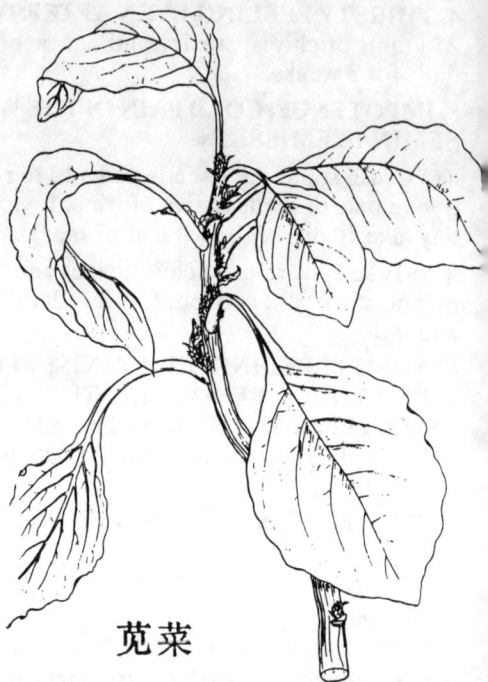

苋菜

The complete stem is used in medicine. It contains protein, fat, carbohydrate, calcium, phosphorous, iron, carotene, vitamins B1, B2 and C, niacin, etc. The flavour is slightly sweet, its nature cool and it affects the lungs and large intestine. It can cool fever, clear the blood and moisten internal organs.

APPLICATIONS

1. JAUNDICE. Take some amaranth and some cuttlefish (squid). Cook together and eat with vegetables for a number of days.

2. DYSENTERY. Take an appropriate quantity of red amaranth, simmer in water and serve. Alternatively after cooking add some honey and serve. Avoid pepper.

3. NOSE BLEEDING, EPITAXIS. Take 30 grams of amaranth root, 15 grams of winter melon rind, 15 grams of cogongrass root and 15 grams of yerhadetajo *(Herba Ecliptae L.)* Simmer in water and serve.

4. ALLERGIC REACTION TO PAINT. Take full stems of amaranth with leaves, simmer in water and wash the affected parts.

5. CENTIPEDE STINGS. Take fresh amaranth leaves, crush and apply to the affected parts.

6. BEE STINGS. Take fresh amaranth plants, crush and apply to the affected place, also crush, obtain juice and drink one cup.

7. CATERPILLAR STINGS THAT FEEL ALTERNATIVELY HOT AND COLD. Take fresh amaranth stems, wash clean and crush to obtain the juice. Serve some of this.

CAUTION: *People suffering from an enlarged spleen should avoid this vegetable.*

CHINESE KALE

Brassica alboglabra L. H. Bailey
(V.G.Sun regards *B.alboglabra* as a variety of
B.oleracia. Herklots p.191)

GAI LAN

Chinese kale, gai lan (mustard indigo), is also called gai lan xin (mustard indigo heart) and ge lan (separate indigo). An annual plant, it has no hair and the stem is vertical with branches. The leaf is egg shaped, the stem thick, the side of the leaf undulating, irregular or slightly saw-toothed. On the stems there are also small leaves that resemble ears. The flower is white or cream. The complete leaf and stem is used in medicine.

芥蓝

It contains protein, fat, carbohydrate, calcium, phosphorous, iron, vitamins B1, B2, C, U, niacin and various amino acids. The flavour is sweet and slightly astringent, its nature is cool and it affects the lungs. It can help neutralize poison, clear the throat and ease breathing problems.

APPLICATIONS

1. COMMON COLD. Take 30 grams of Chinese kale roots, 10 grams of the leaves of the purple perilla *(perilla frutescens var. crispa)*, 10 grams of peppermint leaf and 5 small onions, including the roots. Simmer in water and serve.

2. SORE THROAT. Take 30 grams of Chinese kale roots and 10 salted chinese olives. Simmer together with a quantity of water and drink as a tea.

3. ASTHMATIC COUGH. Take 30 grams of Chinese kale roots, 10 red Chinese dates and 6 grams of dill seed. Simmer in water, dissolve in some sugar and serve.

4. TO PREVENT DIPHTHERIA. Take 30 grams of Chinese kale roots, simmer in water and serve. Eat this two days a week. During a diphtheria epidemic also eat the complete vegetable at frequent intervals.

CAUTION: If suffering from a cold feeling in the stomach and frequently vomiting clear liquid avoid eating this vegetable.

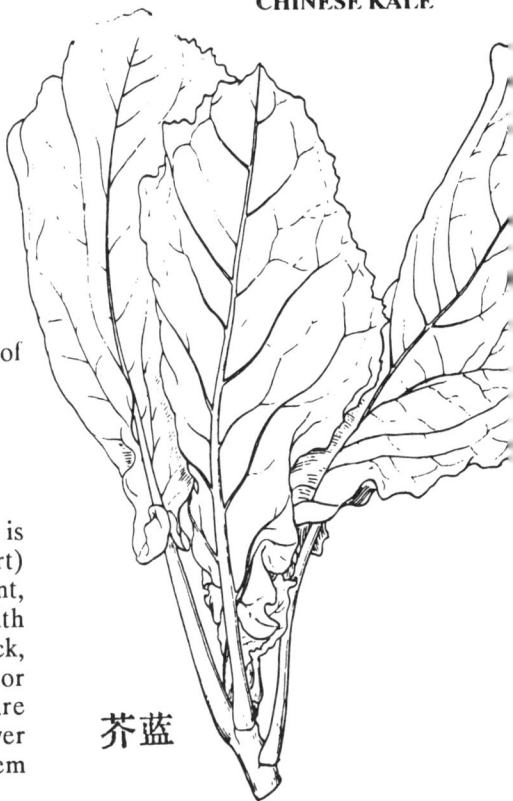

CABBAGE
(CAULIFLOWER can be used in the same way, see notes below.)

Brassica Oleracea L. var. capitata L.

GAN LAN

The cabbage, gan lan (sweet indigo) is also called lan cai (indigo vegetable), xi tu lan (west earth indigo), bao xin cai (wrapped heart vegetable), yang bai cai (foreign white vegetable) and juan xin cai (rolled heart vegetable). The cabbage may live for two years and is often covered with white powder.

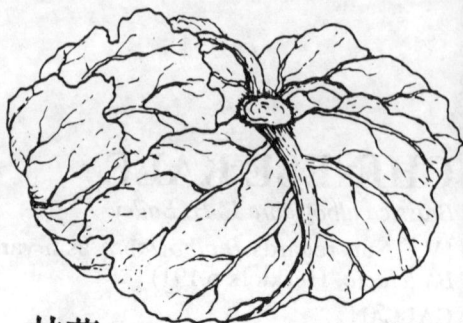

甘蓝

The leaf is large, oval, egg-shaped or round. The leaves are wrapped into a tight ball, the outer leaves green, the inner leaves white. The flower is pale yellow. The leaf is used in medicine.

It contains protein, fat, carbohydrate, calcium, phosphorous, iron, vitamins B1, B2, C, amino acids, etc.. It also contains a substance that affects the thyroid gland. The flavour is sweet-astringent, its nature neither warm nor cool and it affects the spleen and stomach.

It can nourish the bone marrow, "moisten the five internal organs and six viscera", nourish the heart and strengthen bones and sinews.

APPLICATIONS

1. STOMACH ULCERS, DUODENAL ULCER. Take 250 grams of cabbage leaves and boil till partly cooked, then remove from the water. Add a lemon that has been pickled in salt (the longer the better) and a little honey. Return to the pot and simmer until cooked. Eat a little of this a number of times a day and continue this treatment for 15-20 days.

2. STIFF JOINTS, INABILITY TO STRAIGHTEN THE JOINTS. Take 500 grams of cabbage and a hen's foot. Boil into a soup with a little salt and oil. Eat the vegetables and drink the soup.

3. INSOMNIA; RESTLESS SLEEP WITH TOO MANY DREAMS. Take 500 grams of cabbage, 10 grams of lily bulb *(Bulbus Lilii L.)*, 10 grams of lotus seeds and 10 red Chinese dates. First take the lily, lotus seeds and dates and boil till cooked, then add the cabbage and cook. Add a little sesame oil and salt for flavour. Take a small measure several times a day for a week.

4. LEG CRAMPS: Serve cabbage as the main vegetable daily for two weeks. By that time an effect should be noticed.

NOTES.   CABBAGE AND CAULIFLOWER. *The ordinary cabbage and cauliflower are cultivated varieties of the wild cabbage. The cultivated variety of the cabbage has a short stem, the leaf is thick and the leaf stem is short. The leaf may be pale green, deep green or purple, and may be covered with white powder. The leaves wrap around each other to form a ball. The diameter can be up to 300mm.*

The cauliflower leaf is an elongated oval or oval. The stem holds a cluster of edible buds. Both cabbage and cauliflower are grown in Guandong and Guangxi provinces. Their medicinal use is the same.

Cabbage can be pickled in salt or vinegar. Pickled cabbage helps clear the liver and nourishes the gall bladder.

CHINESE CABBAGE

(Often called BAAK CHOI or BOK CHOI in the west, based on the Cantonese pronunciation of BAI CAI, as the word is now written in Pinyin or official Chinese)

Brassica pekinensis (Lour.) Rupr.

BAI CAI

The Chinese cabbage, bai cai (white vegetable), is also called song cai (high vegetable) and huang ya bai (yellow bud white). The plant can live for two years. The leaf is large, and oval or like a reversed egg, the edges are irregular to a greater or less degree. The stem of the leaf is wrapped around the stem of the plant. The flower is pale yellow. There are many cultivated varieties of this vegetable (it can readily be recognised by the broad white leaf stalks topped by green leaves).

白菜

The complete plant is used in medicine. It contains protein, fat, carbohydrate, calcium, phosphorous, iron, vitamins B1, B2, C and niacin.

The flavour is sweet-astringent, its nature cool and it affects the stomach and large intestine. It can cool fever, quench thirst and benefit intestines and stomach.

APPLICATIONS

1. HOT COUGH WITH EXCESSIVE PHLEGM. Take an appropriate quantity of Chinese cabbage, add a little sugar and water, simmer and serve.

2. DERMATITIS FROM PAINT. Crush some Chinese cabbage to obtain the juice and apply this to the affected parts.

3. SMALL FIBRES IN THE EYE. Take a quantity of Chinese cabbage and crush to obtain the juice. Filter this to remove all solids and put 2-3 drops into the eye. The foreign object should be washed out.

4. PETROL POISONING THROUGH INHALATION. Take a quantity of Chinese cabbage, wash clean and crush to obtain the juice and drink as much as possible.

CAUTION. *People suffering from a deficiency of vital energy should avoid eating large quantities of this vegetable.*

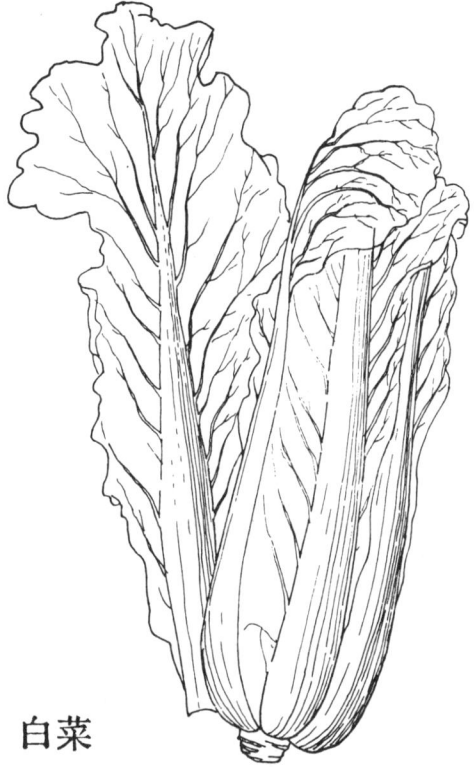

LEAF MUSTARD
INDIAN MUSTARD,
CHINESE MUSTARD

Brassica juncea (L.) Czern & Cosson

GAI CAI

Leaf mustard, gai jie (mustard vegetable), is also called chun bu lao (spring not old) and xue li hong (snow inside red). It is an annual plant. The leaf may be egg-shaped, long oval or inverted egg shape. It usually has an undulating edge with shallow or deep splits. The leaf stem does not wrap around the main stem. The flowers are pale yellow. The seed is round and purple- brown. The complete plant and seeds are used in medicine.

Leaf mustard contains protein, fat, carbohydrate, phosphorous, iron, calcium, carotene, vitamins B1, B2, C, and niacin etc.

芥菜

The flavour of the vegetable is bitter-sweet and astringent, its nature cool. It affects the lungs. The flavour of the seed is bitter, its nature warm, and it affects the lungs and large intestine. Leaf mustard can induce sweating, help the flow of vital energy and clear phlegm. The seeds can warm the lungs, clear phlegm, diminish swelling and ease pain.

APPLICATIONS

1. COMMON COLD WITH HEADACHE; DRY BITTER TASTE IN THE MOUTH.
Take 500 grams of leaf mustard, 100 grams of bean curd, 4 pieces of salted Chinese olive, and 6 grams of fresh ginger. Simmer in water, eat the vegetables while hot and drink the soup to induce sweating.

2. LUNG INFECTIONS. Obtain the juice from year old pickled leaf mustard. Swallow a few drops at a time.

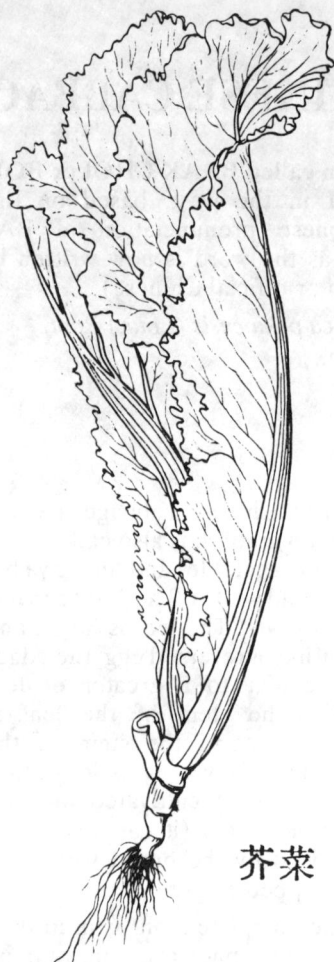

3. GASTRIC DISORDER CAUSING NAUSEA. Grind the leaf mustard seeds into a powder. Take 3 grams in light wine or ginger juice at intervals as needed.

4. HAIR LACKING LIFE OR LUSTRE; EARLY STAGES OF BALDNESS. Take equal quantities of leaf mustard seed and a fresh tuber of *pinellia ternata*. Crush together to a fine consistency and add a little ginger juice. Apply to the scalp twice a day.

5. VOMITING AND DIARRHOEA. Take an appropriate quantity of leaf mustard and crush fine. Take 2 cloves of crushed garlic. Mix together into a paste, heat and apply to the navel, holding it in place with a piece of gauze.

6. DERMATITIS FROM PAINT. Cook some leaf mustard and wash the affected parts with the liquid.

7. HAEMORRHOIDS SWOLLEN AND PAINFUL. Simmer leaf mustard till reduced to a thick liquid and apply warm to the affected parts. Also squat over the steam from the hot liquid.

8. DRY, HOT FEELING WITH EXCESSIVE PHLEGM. Take an appropriate quantity of leaf mustard and rice, boil into a gruel and serve.

CAUTION: *As the seed is warming people suffering from feverish illnesses or heart problems should avoid it.*

NOTES. There are many cultivated varieties of leaf mustard such as la jie cai (peppery leaf mustard), yu jie cai (taro leaf mustard), chun bu lao (spring not old), xue li hong (snow in red), zi tai cai (violet liver-moss leaf mustard) etc. The pickled leaf mustard is sold as Sichuan zha cai (Sichuan pickled mustard), Guangnan tou cai (Guangnan head vegetable), xian suan cai (salted, pickled vegetable), mei cai (plum vegetable) etc.

The seed of the leaf mustard is also called yellow mustard seed, but more usually just gai zi (mustard seed) or gai cai zi (leaf mustard seed). In traditional Chinese medicine it can take the place of white mustard seed. The white mustard seed grows only in Sichuan, Xinjiang and Anhui provinces. Only a few provinces grow the cultivated variety.

FLOWERING CHINESE CABBAGE

BIRD RAPE

Brassica campestris L. var oleifera Dc.
YOU CAI

The flowering cabbage or bird rape, you cai (oil vegetable), is also called cai tai (vegetable moss), you cai tai (oil vegetable moss), and cai xin (vegetable heart). The plant has a life of one or two years. The stem is rough and grows vertically. The leaf has a split appearance and some roughly resemble a violin. The base of the leaf embraces the main stem. The flower is yellow.

油菜

The seed is brown and round. The tender parts of the stem, the leaf and seeds are all used in medicine. The leaf contains protein, fat, carbohydrate, calcium, phosphorous and iron. The seed contains fat, oil and protein.

The flavour of the plant is sweet-astringent, its nature cool and it affects lungs, stomach and great intestine. The flavour of the seed is pungent, its nature warm and it affects the large intestine. The plant can cool fevers, help eliminate poison, disperse blood poisoning and diminish swelling. The seed lubricates the intestines, improves blood circulation and promotes vital energy.

APPLICATIONS

1. VOMITING BLOOD AFTER AN ACCIDENT. Take 500 grams of flowering cabbage, simmer in water, add brown sugar and drink as a tea.

2. DYSENTERY WITH BLEEDING AND STOMACH PAIN. Take fresh flowering cabbage and wash clean, then crush to obtain the juice, add some honey and warm the mixture before serving. Take 30 mls at each serve, 3 times a day.

3. INTESTINAL OBSTRUCTION. Take 100 grams of flowering cabbage seed and 15 grams of fennel seeds. Simmer in water. Divide and take as two serves.

4. BLOOD POISONING AND STOMACH PAINS AFTER GIVING BIRTH. Take 10 grams of flowering cabbage seed, 10 grams of Chinese angelica, and 5 grams of cassia bark. Simmer in water and serve.

5. BOILS ON THE FINGERS. Take some flowering cabbage, wash clean and crush to obtain the juice. Drink as much as desired.

6. MASTITIS. Take some flowering cabbage, wash clean and crush; then apply to the affected parts of the breast.

7. INFECTED BOILS. Take some flowering cabbage, boil in water and wash the affected parts.

CAUTION. *People recovering from measles or scabies or with infected eyes should not eat this vegetable.*

WATERCRESS
Nasturtium officinale R. Br.
XI YANG CAI

Watercress, xi yang cai (west foreign vegetable) is also called ban cai (segment vegetable). A perennial plant that lives in water, it grows to a height of 200-400mm. It is a creeper with many branches which throw out roots from the joints as they go along. The leaves are irregular in shape, with a number on each stem. The smaller leaves form 1-4 pairs along the stem, the end leaf has an irregular or toothed edge. The flowers are white. The whole plant is used in medicine.

西洋菜

Watercress contains Vitamins A, C and D. Its flavour is bitter-sweet, its nature cool and it affects the lungs and bladder. It can moisten the lungs, clear up phlegm, stop coughing, and aid the flow of urine.

APPLICATIONS

1. TUBERCULOSIS. Take 250 grams of watercress and some pork bones, add salt for flavour and simmer into a soup. Divide and drink in 2-3 doses in the course of a day.

2. BURNING FEELING IN THE LUNGS WITH FREQUENT COUGHING. Take 60 grams of watercress and some sugar. Simmer in water and serve.

3. PRURITUS, SKIN IRRITATION. Take an appropriate quantity of watercress, simmer in water and serve frequently.

4. FREQUENT URINATION, URINE CLOUDY, PAIN WHEN URINATING. Take 250 grams of watercress and simmer in water, dissolve some brown sugar into the hot liquid and serve.

CAUTION. *People suffering from a cold empty feeling and lack of strength should be cautious of eating watercress.*

EDITOR'S NOTE. Although watercress is eaten raw in the west, all vegetables in China are boiled due to bacteria in irrigation water.

CELTUCE
or
ASPARAGUS LETTUCE
or
LETTUCE
Lactuca sativa L.
WO JU

(Although the following description refers to celtuce, ordinary lettuce can also be used as mentioned in the notes at the end of this section. Celtuce is a type of lettuce not common in the west but popular in Asia. Celtuce has a thick stem and this is eaten rather than the leaves. Ed.)

Celtuce, wo ju, is also called wo ju sun (lettuce bamboo shoots), wo sun (asparagus lettuce), shen cai (lettuce), bo li sheng cai (glass lettuce), and chun cai (spring vegetable).

莴苣

The plant may live one or two years, the stem is robust and fleshy and can grow up to one metre. The leaves on the base of the plant are long and oval or inverted, egg shaped and wrinkled. The leaves on the stem are oval or egg shaped, and heart shaped where they are attached to the main stem.

The whole plant is used in medicine. It contains protein, fat, carbohydrate, calcium, phosphorous, iron, carotene, vitamins B1, B2, C, niacin, etc. Its flavour is bitter-sweet, its nature cool and it affects the stomach and bladder. It has a beneficial effect upon the "5 internal organs" (a collective term for heart, liver, spleen, lungs and kidneys) and also upon the veins and arteries, and can cool a feverish stomach.

APPLICATIONS

1. INSUFFICIENT BREAST MILK. Take about 500 grams of celtuce and boil into a soup with water. Add an appropriate measure of rice wine or sweet wine and serve, eating the vegetable and drinking the soup.

2. WHEN WORKING IN VERY HOT CONDITIONS OR NEAR A FIRE. Take some celtuce, wash clean and chew as desired.

3. BAD BREATH. Take some celtuce, wash clean and chew.

4. DIFFICULTY IN PASSING URINE; BLOOD IN THE URINE. Take some celtuce, wash clean and chew. In addition it can also be crushed and applied to the navel (using gauze).

5. INSECTS IN THE EAR. Take some celtuce, wash clean and crush to obtain the juice. Put a few drops into the ear.

6. TESTICLES SWOLLEN AND PAINFUL. Take some celtuce seed and crush it to powder. At regular intervals take 10 grams, add water and simmer for 15 minutes, then serve warm.

7. SCARS ON THE HEAD ON WHICH HAIR WILL NOT GROW. Take an equal measure of celtuce seed and rhizome of *Darallia mariesii*, grind together, add a little ginger juice and apply to the affected parts.

CAUTION. *People with a cold feeling in the stomach should be cautious of eating this vegetable.*

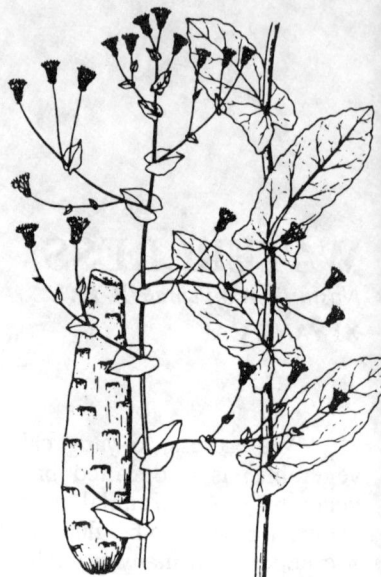

NOTES. There are a number of cultivated varieties of celtuce, such as the following:
1. *Wo ju sun* (Lettuce bamboo shoot). The thick fleshy main stem is eaten.
2. *Qiu ye wo ju* (Ball leaf lettuce). This variety looks like wild cabbage.
3. *Zhou ye wo ju* (Wrinkled leaf celtuce). This is commonly called sheng cai (cos lettuce) or bo li sheng cai (glass lettuce).
4. *Chang ye wo ju* (Long leaf celtuce). This is commonly called chun cai or spring vegetable.
All the above may be used as medicine, the effects being approximately the same.

CHINESE BITTER VEGETABLE
Ixeris denticulata (Houtt.) Stebb.
KU MAI CAI

The Chinese bitter vegetable, ku mai cai, is also called ku cai (bitter vegetable) ku ma cai (bitter numb vegetable), ku ju (endive). An annual upright plant with a hollow stem growing to 900mm. The leaf is a long oval shape with many splits, the sides irregular and toothed. In the lower part of the plant the leaf has a short stem, in the upper part it has no stem and is attached directly to the main stem. The flowers cluster at the top of the plant and are yellow.

The stem, including leaves and flowers are used in medicine. The leaf contains oil, fat, choline, invert sugar, tartaric acid, picrocin acid. The flavour is bitter-sweet, its nature cool, and it affects the heart and large intestine. It can cool fever, help disperse poison, cool the blood and balance moisture in the body.

苦蕒菜

APPLICATIONS
1. ACUTE BACTERIAL DYSENTARY. Take 500 grams of bitter vegetable, simmer in water and serve.

2. ACUTE THROAT INFLAMATION. Take 500 grams of bitter vegetable and 3 grams of rushes (*Juncus effusus L.*) simmer in water and serve.

3. INFLAMATION OF THE APPENDIX. Take 500 grams of bitter vegetable and 60 grams of great blood vine (*Sargentodox cuneata*, known as hong teng in east China and bing land zuan in Guangxi). Simmer in water and serve.

4. BLOOD IN THE URINE. Take 200 grams of bitter vegetable and simmer in water. A little wine can be added before serving.

5. ACUTE YELLOW JAUNDICE AND LIVER INFLAMATION; HEPATITIS. Take 15 grams of bitter vegetable, simmer in water and serve. Another treatment is to take the flowers and seeds, dry in the sun and crush to powder. Twice a day add 6 grams of this to boiled water and serve.

6. BOILS ON THE BACK OF THE NECK. Take fresh bitter vegetable, wash clean and crush to obtain about 200 mls of juice. Add 10 mls of ginger juice and a little

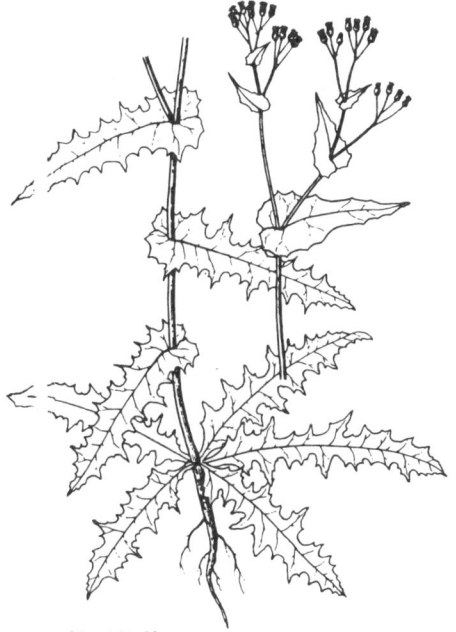

wine if desired. Drink the liquid and spread the sediment on the affected parts as a dressing.

7. PADDY FIELD DERMATITIS. Take fresh bitter vegetable and crush to obtain the juice. Apply this to the affected parts, or simmer to a thick paste and apply this.

8. BEE STING. Take fresh bitter vegetable, crush to obtain the juice and apply this to the affected parts.

CAUTION. *People suffering a cold, empty feeling should avoid eating this vegetable.*

NOTES. The bitter vegetable has a variety called field sowthistle (ye ku mai) which looks similar except that the leaf "ears" are rounded and not pointed. Its medicinal effects are the same.

C A R L A N D CHRYSANTHEMUM
Chrysanthemum segetum L.

TONG HAO CAI

(This is a variety of Chrysanthemum and the young seedlings are eaten as a vegetable. According to Herklots they are sold in the USA under the name of chop suey greens. Ed)

The garland chrysanthemum, tong hao cai, is also called peng hao (fluffy wormwood). It is an annual. The leaf is oval, inverted egg shaped or elongated spoon shape, the edges deeply toothed or split, the base of the leaf wraps around the stem. . The flower is yellow or cream. The complete stem and leaf is used in medicine.

It contains glutamic acid, glutamine, lucid asparagus element, aspartic acid, etc. The flavour is sweet and astringent, its nature warm and it affects the liver and kidneys. It can benefit the kidneys, control the urine, relax internal organs and improve the flow of vital energy (the qi).

蒿蒿菜

APPLICATIONS

1. COUGHING WITH EXCESSIVE PHLEGM. Take 500 grams of the vegetable and 6 grams of dried orange peel, simmer in water and serve.

2. HERNIA SWELLING; PAIN IN THE TESTICLES. Take 500 grams of the vegetable, 10 grams of roasted pangolin (scaly ant eater) scales (stocked by Chinese herbalists), 10 grams of fennel seeds and 5 kernels of mango *Mangifera indica L.*). Simmer in water and serve.

3. FREQUENT NEED TO URINATE DURING THE NIGHT. Take 500 grams of the vegetable and 50 grams of black soyabeans. First take the black soyabeans and stir-fry till cooked. Add water and simmer till the beans are soft and easy to chew. Add the vegetable, plus a little oil (peanut oil) and salt for flavour and simmer till cooked. Eat the vegetable and drink the soup.

4. BED WETTING AND PANT'S WETTING IN SMALL CHILDREN. Take an appropriate amount of the vegetable, add a piece of tang jiao fish *(Clarias fuscus L.))* and simmer in water. Add oil and salt for flavour and serve.

SPINACH
Spinacia oleracea L.
BO CAI

Spinach, bo cai, is also called bo ling, bo ling cai, .cai, and bo si cai. It is an annual vegetable with smooth leaves. The root is round and tapering, the stem straight with an open centre. The leaf is spear shaped, the edge wavy or with a few teeth. The complete stem and leaf are used in medicine.

It contains protein, fat, carbohydrate, calcium, phosphorous, iron, carotene, vitamin C, niacin, as well as a small amount of vitamins B1 and B2. The leaf also contains folic acid and amino acids, etc. The flavour is astringent, its nature neither warm nor cool and it affects the stomach and large intestine. It can be used to treat a deficiency of yin (see below), nourish the blood, and act upon the intestines.

APPLICATIONS

1. CHRONIC THIRST; DIABETES WITH POLYDIPSIA. Take an equal measure of spinach root and chicken gizzard, crush to a fine consistency. For each serve add 3 grams to rice gruel and serve 3 times a day.

菠菜

2. HABITUAL CONSTIPATION. Take an appropriate quantity of spinach and rice. Cook to a gruel and serve.

3. LACK OF IRON LEADING TO POOR BLOOD; ANEMIA. Take 250 grams of spinach and 50 grams of pork liver. Boil into a soup, add a little oil and salt for flavour and serve.

CAUTION. *Persons suffering from stomach pains or watery thin motions should avoid this vegetable.*

DEFICIENCY OF YIN is indicated by a dry cough, blood in the spit, mild fever in the afternoon or evening, night sweat, dry throat or mouth, lumbago, spermatorrhoea, abnormal menstruation, dizziness, vertigo, hot palms of hands and feet, etc.

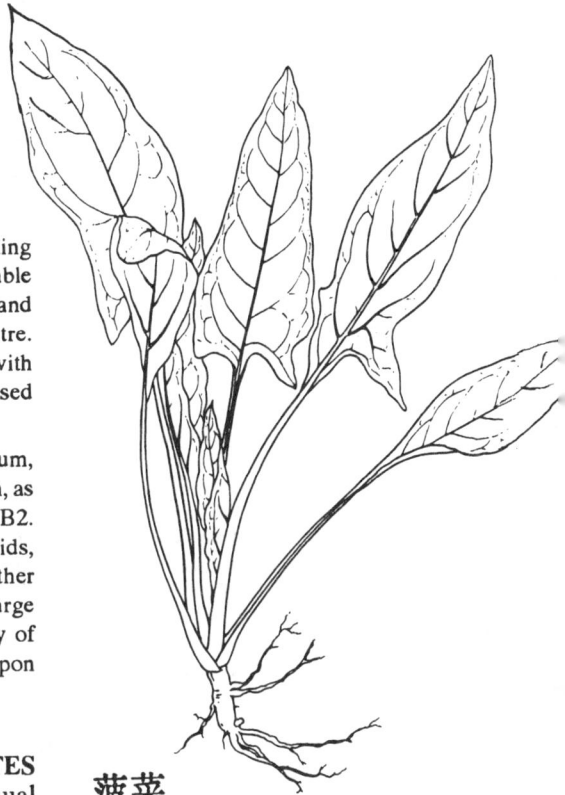

LEAF-BEET
or
SWISS CHARD
Beta vulgaris L. var. cicla L.
JUN DA CAI

Leaf-beet or Swiss Chard, jun da cai, is also called hou pi cai (thick skin vegetable), niu pi cai (cattle skin vegetable), and zhu mu cai (pig mother vegetable). The plant lives for two years and is smooth, without hair. The roots are not large and are branching. The leaf is oval, smooth edged or with a slightly undulating edge and a long leaf stem. The flowers are in clusters and the seed is red-brown.

Stem, leaves and seeds are all used in medicine. The plant contains protein, fat, carbohydrate, calcium, phosphorous, iron, vitamins B1, B2, C, carotene and niacin.

莙达菜

The flavour is bitter-sweet and astringent, its nature cool, and it affects the stomach and large intestine. It can calm fever, cool the blood, moisten the intestines and neutralize poison.

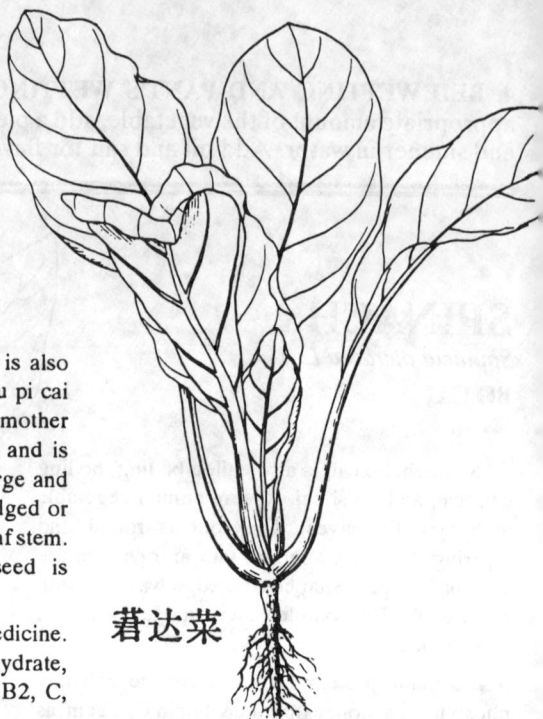

APPLICATIONS

1. HIGH FEVER. Take a quantity of the fresh vegetable, wash clean, crush to obtain the juice and serve.

2. INFLAMATION OF THE INTESTINES; DYSENTERY. Take an appropriate quantity of the vegetable, add water, boil into a gruel and serve.

3. HAEMORRHOIDS, SORE AND BLEEDING. Simmer the complete vegetable into a thick juice with water and wash the affected parts, and also squat over the steaming liquid.

4. BOILS, INFECTED. Take a quantity of the vegetable, wash clean and crush to obtain the juice. Drink this frequently, and apply the sediment to the affected parts.

5. ACNE; TO MOISTEN THE SKIN. Soak the seeds in vinegar for 3-5 days. Wipe the vinegar on the face once or twice a day.

CAUTION: *If suffering from an empty, cold feeling, stomach pains or watery motions avoid eating this vegetable.*

NOTES. The cultivated variety of this plant is frequently seen in the south and south-west part of China. The stem may be red or purple-red, with a bright surface. The red variety is commonly called flame vegetable and is grown both for food and as an ornamental. The medicinal value of all varieties are the same.

(Leaf beet or Swiss chard is related to common beetroot but does not have the bulbous root, and is eaten as a green. Ed.)

COFFEE SENNA

Cassia occidentalis L.

WANGJIANG NAN

Wang jiang nan (gaze river south) is also called yang jiao cao (sheep horn vegetable), and tou yun cao (head dizzy vegetable). It is a shrub or small tree growing to a height of 1-2 metres.

望江南

It has compound leaves which grow opposite each other, 3-5 pairs on a stalk. The leaves are egg shaped to oval, pointed at the end. The leaf stem is swollen at the point where it joins the stalk. The flower is yellow.

The seeds are found in a long, narrow, flat pod, 30-40 in each pod. Stem, leaves and seeds are used in medicine. The stem contains tannin, fat, oil and glue. The seed contains emodin, tannin, fat oil, poison protein etc. The leaf contains a small reserve of potassium oxide anthraquinone.

The flavour of the plant is bitter-sweet, its nature cool. It is slightly poisonous, and affects the liver and stomach. It can cool fever, calm the liver, brighten the eye, neutralize poison and moisten the intestines.

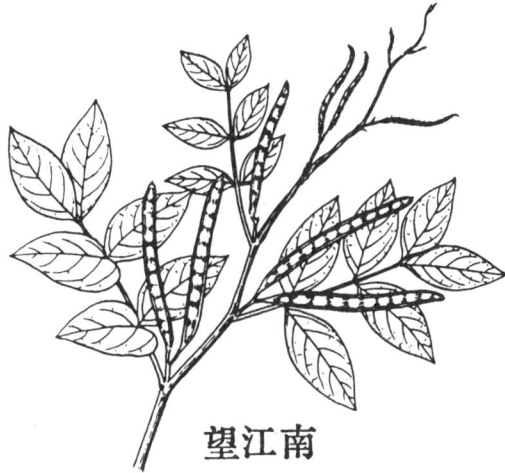

APPLICATIONS (note caution below)

1. **STUBBORN HEADACHE.** Take 30 grams of leaves, 60 grams of lean pork and a little salt for flavouring. Simmer in water and serve.

2. **HIGH BLOOD PRESSURE; CHRONIC GASTROENTERITIS; CHRONIC CONSTIPATION.** Take 15-30 grams of the seeds and roast them. Crush, then simmer in water and serve. Another treatment is to pour boiling water on the crushed roasted seeds and drink the liquid in place of tea. Continue for 2 weeks.

3. **COUGHING WITH HOT PHLEGM.** Take 30 grams of the complete plant, simmer in water and serve.

4. **BLOOD IN THE URINE.** Take 30 grams of the complete plant, simmer in water and serve.

5. **CONJUNCTIVITIS; STOMACH INFLAMATION; INFLAMED URINARY PASSAGE, LEUCORRHOEA, DYSENTERY.** Take 15-30 grams of fresh seed, crush, simmer in water and serve.

6. **SORES IN THE MOUTH.** Take 30 grams of fresh seed, crush and simmer to a thick juice. Rinse the mouth with this a number of times a day.

7. **INFLAMATION OF THE BREASTS; MASTITIS; FOLLICULITUS, BOILS IN THE NOSE.** Take 30-60 grams of the whole plant or 15-30 grams of the crushed seed, simmer in water and serve.

8. **INFECTED AND INFLAMED SORES.** Take sun-dried leaves and crush to powder, mix with a little vinegar and apply as a dressing. For weeping sores a gap will be made in the centre of the dressing to allow the sore to discharge pus. Put 3 grams of the powder in yellow wine and take this twice a day.

CAUTION: Because of the poisonous nature of this plant caution should be observed in its use, and internal treatment should be of a short duration.

(According to Usher, A Dictionary of Plants Used by Man, p.129, the plant gets its common name from the fact that it has been used as a coffee substitute, called Negro Coffee or Mogdad coffee. Ed.)

CHINESE WOLFBERRY
Lycium chinense Mill.
GOU QI CAI

The Chinese wolfberry, gou qi cai (wofberry vegetable) is also called gou qi (wolfberry), niu ji li (cow auspicious strength), gou ya zi (dog tooth), gou nai zi (dog's udder), gou qi miao (wolfberry seedling), and gou qi tou (wolfberry head). It is a shrub with many small branches and usually has thorns. The leaves are often in clusters of 2-4, and are egg shaped, oval or like a spinning top. The flower is pale purple. The fruit is red when ripe. The leaf, root, bark of the root and fruit are all used in medicine.

The fruit contains glycine, carotene, vitamins B1, B2, c, niacin, etc. The flavour of the complete plant is bitter-sweet, its nature cool, and it affects liver, kidneys and lower lungs.

枸杞菜

APPLICATIONS

1. DIABETES. Take 60 grams of wolfberry leaves, simmer in water to a thick juice and serve as a tea.

2. ACUTE CONJUNCTIVITIS. Take 60 grams of wolfberry leaves and a hen egg and simmer with water into a soup. Add a little salt and oil for flavour and serve once a day.

3. ACHING KIDNEYS AND STOMACH WITH LACK OF STRENGTH; INTERNAL STRAINS. Take 250 grams of wolfberry leaves, a sliced sheep's kidney, 60 grams of rice and 10 spring onions. Cook with water to a stew, add a little oil and salt for flavour and serve.

4. FAILING VISION; NIGHT BLINDNESS. Take 60 grams of wolfberry leaves and 60 grams of pork liver. Boil into a soup, add a little oil and salt for flavour and serve.

5. INFLAMATION OF THE NOSE AND SINUS; SINUSITIS. Take 60 grams of wolfberry root and 10 grams of licorice root. Simmer in water and drink as a tea for one month.

6. TOOTHACHE. Take 60 grams of wolfberry root, simmer in water and serve.

7. MIGRAINE. Take 60 grams of wolfberry root and a hen or duck egg. Simmer in water to a soup, eat the egg and drink the soup.

8. LEUCORRHOEA. Take 60 grams of wolfberry root and 60 grams of lean pork. Boil into a soup, add a little oil (peanut oil) and salt for flavour, eat the meat and drink the soup.

9. HAEMORRHOIDS SORE AND SWOLLEN. Take an appropriate quantity of the stem and leaves of the wolfberry, simmer with water and wash the affected parts, and also squat over the steaming liquid.

10. PALPITATIONS OF THE HEART WITH THIRST; ANXIETY. Simmer the root of the wolfberry in water and drink as a tea.

11. PALPITATIONS OF THE HEART WITH THIRST AND HECTIC FEVER IN SMALL CHILDREN. Take either the roots or the stem and leaf, simmer in water and drink as a tea.

CAUTION. *While being treated with this plant avoid cow's milk or other dairy products.*

NOTES. The root, bark and the fruit may be equally used in medicine. The root bark is called di gu pi (earth bone skin), its flavour is bitter-sweet, its nature cool. It helps in the treatment of inflamed lungs, hot coughing, hectic fever due to a yin deficiency, feverish thirst, lowers high temperature, etc.

The fruit is called gou qi zi (wolfberry seed), its flavour is sweet, its nature neither warm nor cool. It nourishes the liver and kidneys, promotes virility and vital energy and brightens the eye. Frequent use improves liver, kidney, lack of strength, impotence, etc.

CLUSTER MALLOW

Malva crispa L.
DONG JUI

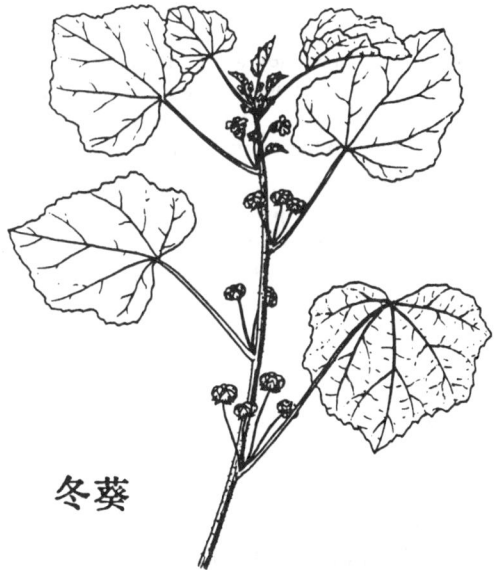

冬葵

The cluster mallow, dong kui, (winter big flower), is also called dong xian cai (winter amaranth vegetable), dong han cai (winter cool vegetable) hua hua cai (slippery, slippery vegetable), and qi cai ba ba ye (this refers to the fact that the roots of the cluster mallow have a similar medicinal effect to that of the roots of milk vetch). The plant lives for two years, the stem is vertical and covered with star like hair.

The leaf is round, with 5-7 shallow splits and a long stem. The flowers are in clusters and are pink. The fruit is round and flat with 2-4 small round seeds. Stem, leaf and seed are all used in medicine.

The seed contains fat, oil and protein. The flower contains mucilage. The root, stem and leaf contain high mallow acid, monosaccharide, sucrose, maltose, starch, etc. The flavour of the seed is sweet, its nature cool and it affects the large intestine, kidneys and bladder. The effects of the stem, leaf, seed and root are generally the same. They can benefit the urine, encourage the flow of breast milk, moisten the intestines and bowels.

APPLICATIONS

1. DIFFICULTY IN PASSING MOTIONS; CONSTIPATION; BLOATED FEELING. Take 60 grams of seeds, simmer in water and serve.

2. LACK OF BREAST MILK; BREASTS SWOLLEN AND PAINFUL. Take 60 grams of seeds and stir fry until fragrant. Add equal quantities of wine and water, simmer and serve.

3. DIFFICULTY IN HAVING CHILDREN DUE TO A WEAK, SHRUNKEN WOMB. Take 60 grams of the whole plant, simmer in water and serve.

4. ASTHENIA, LACK OF STRENGTH WITH DROPSY, OEDEMA. Take 30 grams of the root of the plant, 6 grams of white pepper and some pork spleen. Simmer into a soup and serve.

5. SCORPION BITE; INSECT STINGS. Take some leaves, wash clean and crush to obtain the juice. Drink this and apply the sediment to the wound.

CAUTION. *Pregnant women and people suffering from semi-liquid motions should avoid this vegetable.*

WATER SPINACH
HOLLOW VEGETABLE
SWAMP CABBAGE
Ipomoea aquatica Forsk.
WENG CAI

The water spinach, weng cai, is also called kong xin cai (hollow vegetable), weng cai (luxuriant vegetable), and tong cai (penetrate vegetable). An annual plant that lives in moist areas or in the water. The stem is round and hollow and has joints from which roots appear.

The leaves may be egg shaped, elongated egg shape or like a spinning top, the edges smooth or with a slight wave. The flower is white, pink or violet. The fruit is egg shaped or round. the whole plant is used in medicine. It contains protein, fat, carbohydrate, calcium, phosphorous, iron, vitamins B1, B2, C, niacin, etc.

The flavour is insipid, its nature cool and it affects the stomach and large intestine. It can cool fever, disperse poison, moisten the internal organs and stop bleeding.

蕹菜

APPLICATIONS

1. TO TREAT POISONING FROM GELSEMIUM ELEGANS. Take 500 grams each of water spinach root and ji xue cao (*Centella asiatica*) (also called lei gong gen, -Thunder God root) and beng da wan (break great bowl). Wash clean, crush to obtain juice and serve.

2. HEADACHE WITH PUS FLOWING FROM THE EAR; OTORRHOEA. Take about 100 grams of water spinach and 100 grams of dog meat. Simmer in water and serve. Continue the treatment for a number of days.

3. NOSE BLEEDING. Take an appropriate amount of water spinach and sugar, crush together, pour on boiling water and serve.

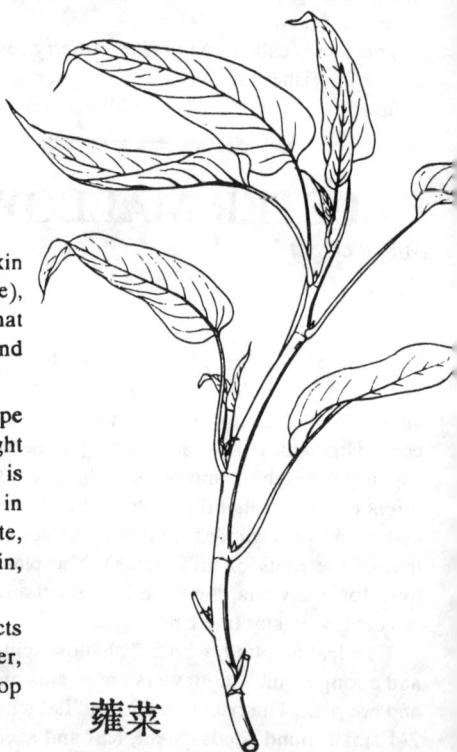

46

4. URINE MUDDY; BLOOD IN URINE AND FAECES. Take a quantity of water spinach, wash clean and crush to obtain the juice. Mix in a little honey and serve.

5. HAEMORRHOIDS SWOLLEN AND PAINFUL. Take an appropriate amount of water spinach, add some salt and crush. Apply to the affected place.

6. TOOTHACHE. Take 100 grams of water spinach root, add equal quantities of water and vinegar and simmer. Use this as a gargle.

7. DIFFICULTY IN PASSING URINE AFTER WALKING LONG DISTANCES ON HOT DAYS. Simmer a quantity of water spinach root in water and serve.

8. BOILS. Take an appropriate quantity of water spinach, 2 pieces of star anise (*Illicium anisatum*) and some brown sugar. Crush together and apply to the affected parts.

9. CENTIPEDE STINGS. Take some water spinach and salt, rub to a paste in the hands and apply to the affected part.

CAUTION: *Persons suffering from a cold feeling in the stomach should avoid this vegetable.*

NOTES. The variety of water spinach that grows in the water is called shui weng, the variety that grows on moist ground is known as han weng.

CELERY

Apium graveolens L.

HAN QIN

早芹

The celery, han qin, (dryland celery) is also called qin cai (celery vegetable), and yang qin cai (foreign celery). The plant lives for one or two years and has a fragrant smell. The stem is vertical, with distinct grooves and ridges running down it. The leaves are feathery with a number of splits in them. The fruit is smooth, round or oval with blunt angles. The complete plant is used as medicine.

It contains protein, fat, carbohydrate, calcium, phosphorous, iron as well as a small amount of vitamins B1, B2, C, volatile oils, carotene and niacin. The flavour is bitter-sweet, its nature cool and it affects the stomach and liver. It helps settle an inflamed liver, dispels wind and moistens the internal organs.

APPLICATIONS

1. HIGH BLOOD PRESSURE; HIGH CHOLESTEROL LEVELS. Take some fresh celery, wash clean and crush to obtain the juice, take 40 mls each serve, 3 times a day. Honey or sugar can be added if desired.

2. HOT FLUSHES IN A WOMAN; UTERINE BLEEDING. Take 60 grams of celery and 30 grams of motherwort (*Leonurus heterophyllus*). Simmer in water and serve.

3. CHYLURIA, MILKY URINE. Take 100 grams of celery stalks, the green ones are best, add 500 grams of water and simmer till reduced to 200 ml. Take both in the morning and evening on an empty stomach for 3-7 days.

CAUTION: *People suffering from scabies should avoid this vegetable.*

WATER DROPWORT
WATER CELERY
Oenanthe Javanica (Bl.) DC.
SHUI QIN

Water dropwort, shui qin, is also called shui qin cai (water celery vegetable). It is a perennial aquatic plant of a creeping nature with roots on each joint in the lower part of the plant. The leaves on the lower part of the stalk have a short stem, those at the end of the stalk do not. The fruit is oval or conical.

The whole plant is used in medicine. It contains volatile oils, water dropwort essential element, a variety of animo acids, etc. The flavour is bitter-sweet, its nature cool and it afects lungs and stomach. It can cool a fever, disperse poison, clear the lungs and moisten the internal organs.

水芹

APPLICATIONS

1. PAIN WHEN URINATING. Take some root section of water dropwort, wash clean, crush to obtain the juice and serve. Drink half a bowl twice a day.

2. BLOOD IN THE MOTIONS. Take an appropriate quantity of water dropwort, wash clean and crush to obtain half a bowl of juice. Add a little brown sugar and serve.

3. YELLOW JAUNDICE. Take 60 grams of fresh water dropwort root and lower part of the plant, 30 grams of day lily and 100 grams of lean pork. Add some salt for flavour, boil in water and serve.

4. TOOTHACHE. Take 60 grams of the root and lower part of the water dropwort and a duck egg. Simmer with water, then drink the soup and eat the egg.

5. MUMPS. Take an appropriate quantity of fresh water dropwort and crush to obtain the juice. Add some vinegar and serve, also rub the affected parts with the liquid.

CAUTION: *People suffering a cold, empty feeling in the stomach should avoid this vegetable.*

WATERSHIELD

Brasenia schreberi J.F. Gmel.

CHUN CAI

Watershield, chun cai, is a perennial water plant. The stem is small and has a creeping nature. The leaf floats on the water and is round or oval with smooth edges, the upper surface is green, the lower one indigo-green and both sides are smooth. The stem is 250- 400mm long and covered with flexible hairs. Both stem and pedical contain a glue-like substance.

莼菜

The single flower has a diameter of 10-20mm and is dark purple. The nut is egg shaped. The whole plant is used in medicine. It contains Vitamin B12 and polysaccharide.

The flavour is sweet, its nature cool, and it affects the liver and spleen. It can cool a fever, promote diuresis, diminish swelling and neutralize poison.

APPLICATIONS

1. CHRONIC THIRST (OFTEN RELATED TO DIABETES). Take an appropriate quantity of the whole plant and some crucian carp fish. Add salt for flavour and cook into a soup. Drink twice a day for about a fortnight.

2. ACUTE YELLOW JAUNDICE WITH LIVER INFLAMATION; HEPATITIS. Take 30-60 grams of the whole plant, simmer in water, add a little sugar and serve.

3. BOILS. Take an appropriate quantity of the plant, crush and apply to the affected parts.

CAUTION: *Persons suffering from a cold, empty feeling in the stomach and spleen should avoid this plant.*

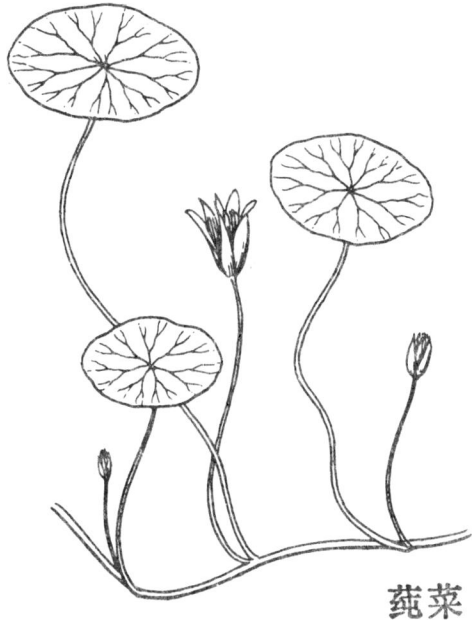

DAYLILY
Hemerocallis citrina Baroni
HUANG HUA CAI

The day lily, huang hua cai (yellow flower vegetable) is also called jin zhen cai (gold needle vegetable), ning meng xuan cao (lemon tawny day lily), wang you (forget worry) and yi nan (appropriate man). It is a perennial plant, the root fleshy and swollen. The leaves are long and narrow and in groups of 7-20. The flower is pale yellow in the wild, but there are many cultivated varieties. The dry flower bud and the roots are used in medicine.

The daylily contains protein, fat, carbohydrates, calcium, phosphorous, iron, carotene, vitamins B1, B2, niacin, etc. The flavour of the flower is sweet, its nature cool, and it affects the lungs and large intestines. The flavour of the root is bitter, its nature cool and it affects the spleen and lungs. The flower benefits the internal organs and chest.

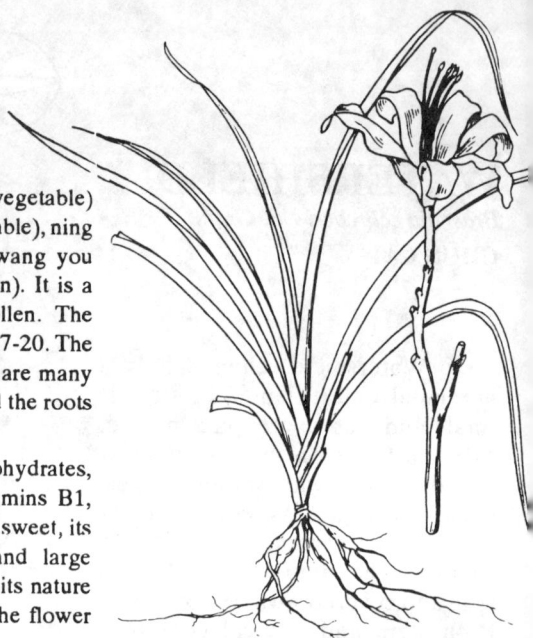

黄花菜

APPLICATIONS

1. HIGH BLOOD PRESSURE. Take 30 grams of daylily root and 30 grams of water chestnuts. Simmer with water and drink as a tea.

2. DYSENTERY. Take 30 grams of daylily and 50 grams of brown sugar. Simmer in water and serve.

3. YELLOW JAUNDICE AFFECTING THE COLOUR OF THE WHOLE BODY. Take 30 grams of daylily or 30 grams of the root, simmer in water and serve. Some lean pork can be added and the liquid simmered to a soup.

4. BLOOD IN THE FAECES AND URINE. Take 30 grams of daylily and 10 grams of wood ear fungus (*auricularia auricula-judae*). Simmer in water, add a little sugar and serve.

5. PROLAPSE OF THE RECTUM. Take 30 grams of daylily, 30 grams of wood ear fungus (*auricularia auricula-judae*) and some sugar. Simmer in water and serve.

6. HOARSE SPEECH. Take 30 grams of daylily, simmer in water, add honey and hold in the throat for as long as possible.

7. MENSTRUATION AHEAD OF TIME. Take 30 grams of daylily and 100 grams of celery, simmer in water and serve.

8. INFLAMED THROAT IN A BABY CAUSING DIFFICULTY IN BREAST FEEDING. Take 10 grams of daylily and simmer in water to obtain half a cup of liquid, add honey to the liquid and serve.

9. DROPSY, OEDEMA. Dry the root of the daylily in the sun and grind into a powder. Take 6 grams of the powder and add this to rice soup. Do this twice a day.

CAUTION. *In medicine the flower is used in dried form. It is best not to use fresh flowers. Do not eat a large quantity of the root, 30 grams a day should be the maximum allowed.*

SWORD FLOWER
Hylocerus undatus (Haw.) Britt et Rose
JIAN HUA

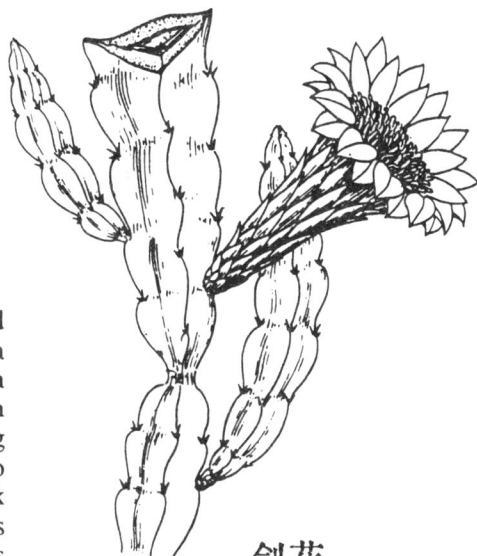

The sword flower, jian hua (sword flower) is also called liang tian chi hua (Celestial ruler flower), ba wang hua (despot flower) and fan gui lian (foreign devil lotus). It is a perennial climbing cactus with aerial roots that will cling to rocks, trees or walls. The stem is dark green with many branches, and in cross section has 3 angles. The angular ridges are wavy and have spines. The flower is very large, about 300mm long and white in colour. It has an oval red fruit. Both flower and stem are used in medicine.

剑花

The flower contains a mucilage like substance, protein, sugar etc. The flavour is sweet, its nature neither warm nor cool and it affects the lungs and stomach. It can act as a tonic on the spleen and stomach, moisten the lungs and ease coughing.

APPLICATIONS

1. PULMONARY TUBERCULOSIS. Take 30 grams of the flower, add an appropriate amount of crystal sugar, simmer in water and serve.

2. DRY HOT COUGH. Take 30 grams of the flower, 6 grams of dried orange peel and a little white or brown sugar, simmer in water and serve.

3. STOMACH ULCER, DUODENAL ULCER; PEPTIC ULCER. Take 60 grams of the stem or 30 grams of the flower, 30 grams of chuan po shi, cudrania root (*Cudrania pubescens*) and 15 grams of licorice root. Simmer in water and serve.

4. MUMPS; SWELLINGS FROM FALLS AND ACCIDENTS. Take some of the stem, remove the spines and crush, then apply to the affected place.

5. BURNS AND SCALDS. Crush some stem and apply the juice to the affected parts.

CAUTION. *People suffering from accumulation of phlegm should avoid eating this plant.*

51

ROSE OF SHARON
Hibiscus syriacus L.
MU JIN HUA

木槿花

The rose of sharon, mu jin hua, is also called bai sang hua (white mulberry flower) and zi sang hua (mauve mulberry flower). It is a shrub with an egg shaped or oval leaf, usually with 3 shallow splits on each side like an irregular saw tooth edge. The single flower is mauve, but may be also white or pink.

The flower, stem, leaf and root are all used in medicine. The flower contains a glutinous substance, saponin, and isovitexin. The flavour of the flower is sweet-astringent, its nature neither warm nor cool, and it affects lungs, spleen and large intestine. It can cool fever, cool the blood and moisten internal organs. The stem can control phlegm and ease coughing.

APPLICATIONS

1. DYSENTERY. Take 30 grams of flowers, simmer in water, add honey and serve an appropriate quantity at regular intervals.

2. VOMITING BLOOD, BLOOD IN THE FAECES. Take 10 flowers and some sugar, simmer in water and serve before meals twice a day.

3. GASTRIC DISORDERS WITH NAUSEA, VOMITING. Dry the flowers in the shade then grind to a powder. Every day add 3-5 grams to rice soup and serve.

4. CHRONIC TRACHEITIS. Take 120 grams of the stems, add water and simmer to 100 mls of liquid. Divide into two serves and take in the course of a day.

5. CHRONIC THIRST. Take 60 grams of the root, simmer in a quantity of water and drink in place of tea.

6. LEUCORRHOEA. Take 10 flowers or 30-60 grams of the root and 120 grams of pork rib bones or backbone. Simmer in water and serve.

7. HAEMORRHOIDS SWOLLEN AND PAINFUL. Take a quantity of the stem and leaves, simmer in water and use the liquid to wash the affected part. Also squat over the steaming liquid.

8. TINEA CIRCINATA ON THE HEAD. Take some bark of the stem or the root, dry and grind to a powder. Add an appropriate amount of vinegar and boil into a paste. Apply this to the affected parts.

9. BOILS. Take the flowers or leaves, crush to a paste and apply as a dressing to the affected parts.

CAUTION. *Persons suffering from a cold, empty feeling in the spleen and stomach should avoid this plant.*

CORDATE TELOSMA
Telosma cordata (burm. f.) Merr.
YE LAI XIANG

The cordate telosma, ye lai xiang (night come fragrant), is also called ye xiang hua (night fragrant flower), qian li xiang (thousand li flower) and ye lan xiang (night orchid fragrant). It is a vine like shrub. The stalk is flexible and covered with fine hairs. The leaf is a wide heart shape and thin. The flowers grow in clusters of up to 30 and are fragrant and yellow-green. The seed is a wide egg shape, the top having white fine hairs. Both flower and leaf are used in medicine.

The flower contains a fragrant oil, its flavour is sweet and insipid, its nature neither warm nor cool and it affects the liver. The flower can clear the liver and brighten the eyes.

夜来香

APPLICATIONS

1. RED EYES; AVERSION TO LIGHT; BLURRED VISION. Take 30 grams of the flowers and an appropriate amount of pork liver. Boil into a soup, add a little salt for flavour and serve.

2. SORES AND BOILS WHICH DO NOT CLOSE UP. Crush a quantity of the leaf and apply to the affected parts as a dressing.

WINTER MELON
WAX GOURD
Benincasa hispida (Thunb.) Cogn.
DONG GUA

The winter melon, dong gua (winter melon), is also called bai gua (white melon) and dong gua (east melon). The vine is an annual. The stem has hairs on it. The leaf is circular with 5-7 splits and both sides are covered with short stiff hair. The flower is yellow. The fruit is large and cylindrical or round, the surface has hairs and a white waxy powder. The flesh is thick and white. The seed is egg shaped and white.

冬瓜

The melon flesh, skin and seed are all used in medicine. The melon contains protein, fat, sugar, calcium, phosphorous, iron, carotene, vitamins B1, B2, C, niacin, etc. The seed contains saponin, urea, citrulline, oleic acid, linoleic acid, palmic acid, etc.

The flavour of flesh, skin and seed is sweet and insipid, their nature cool. They affect lungs, spleen and heart. The flesh promotes diuresis , diminishes phlegm, cools fever and dispenses poison. The skin cools fever, benefits the urine and diminishes swelling. The seed cools fever, clears phlegm, and clears pus from boils and sores.

APPLICATIONS

1. DROPSY. Take 1-1.5 kilos of winter melon, add 250 grams of dried meat and boil till cooked. Divide into four portions and eat in the course of a day.

2. DIABETES. Take a winter melon, about 2.5 kilos, cut off the top and scoop out the seeds and pulp. Place inside 30 grams of huang lian powder (Chinese golden thread, *Coptis chinensis*). Replace the top of the melon and secure in place with skewers. Place the melon in a charcoal fire and let it cook, then squeeze the flesh to obtain the juice. Divide into 3 serves and take in the course of a day.

3. INFLAMATION OF THE KIDNEYS WITH DROPSY; NEPHRITIS. Take 30-60 grams of winter melon skin and an equal quantity of bai mao gen (white cogongrass rhizomes, *Imperata cylindrica*) and simmer in water. Take a small amount 3 times a day.

4. THIRST ASSOCIATED WITH DROPSY; INADEQUATE FLOW OF URINE; OLIGURIA. Take 500 grams of the pith of the melon, simmer in water and serve as a tea.

5. NETTLE RASH, URTICARIA. Take an appropriate quantity of melon skin, simmer in water and serve as a tea.

6. CLOUDY URINE IN MALES; LEUCORRHOEA. Dry winter melon seeds in the sun, then grind to a powder. At regular intervals add 10 grams to rice soup and serve.

7. PULMONARY ABSCESS; INFLAMED BREAST AND STOMACH WITH LIQUID IN THE LUNGS. Take 30 grams each of winter melon seed, common reed rhizhome *(Rhizoma Phragmitis)* and Job's tears *(Coix lachryma-jobi L.)*, 15 grams of honeysuckle flowers and 10 grams of the Chinese bellflower (*Platycodon grandiflorum*). Simmer in water and serve.

8. FOOD POISONING FROM FISH. Crush a winter melon to obtain the juice and drink this.

CAUTION: *If suffering from a cold, empty feeling in the stomach avoid this vegetable.*

PUMPKIN
Cucurbita moschata (Duch. ex Lam.)
Duch. ex Poir.

NAN GUA

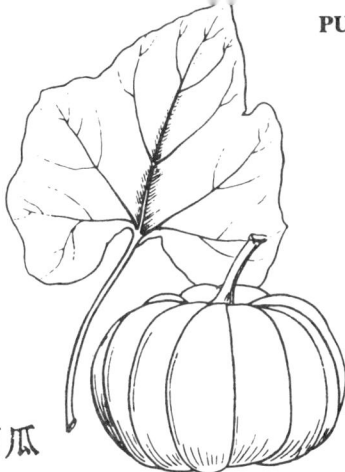

南瓜

The pumpkin, nan gua (south melon) is also called fan gua (foreign melon) and fan gua (food melon). It is an annual vine and the stem is covered with short, stiff hairs. The leaf may be circular, eggshaped, five cornered or with five shallow splits. The flower is yellow.

The fruit is very large and may be cylindrical, like a flattened ball, round or gourd shaped. It usually has a number of deep vertical grooves in it and when ripe is covered with a white powder. It may be red-brown or yellow-brown, with thick flesh. The seeds are pale grey and have a slight fringe. The fruit, seed, pith and stem are all used in medicine.

The pumpkin contains protein, fat, sugar, calcium, phosphorous, iron, carotene, vitamins B1, B2, C, niacin, citrulline, arginine, trigonelline, etc. The seed contains fat oil, protein, vitamins A, B1, B2, C, carotene, etc.

The flavour of the pumpkin is sweet, its nature warm and it affects the spleen and stomach. The flavour of the seed is sweet, its nature neither warm nor cool. The pumpkin can nourish the spleen, warm the stomach, and nourish internal organs. The seed can help expel internal parasites.

APPLICATIONS

1. HOLLOW COUGH. Take 250 grams of pumpkin, add an appropriate quantity of crystal sugar, simmer in water and serve.

2. ROUNDWORM. Eat raw pumpkin, 500 grams for adults and proportionally less for children. Take a little every 2 hours, and also take a laxative. Repeat the treatment for a second day.

3. TAPEWORM. Take 60-120 grams of pumpkin seeds, remove skins and eat. Another treatment is to roast the seeds and grind to a powder and eat in the morning on an empty stomach. 30-60 minutes later take 30-60 grams of bing lang (betelnut *Areca catechu L.*). Simmer in water and serve. If the patient has not had motions within 2 hours, 6-10 grams of glauber's salt may be taken in hot water. After motions something puffy and soft may be felt in the area of the anus, defecate in warm water to wash out the tapeworm.

4. SCHISTOSOMIASIS. Take pumpkin seeds, discard the skins and crush to a powder. Take 240 grams a day divided into 3 serves and continue the treatment for a month.

5. PROLAPSE OF THE UTERUS, METROPTOSIS. Take 5 stems of pumpkin from where they attach to the fruit, a total of about 100 grams, 10 fruit stems of eggplant and a hen. Pluck and clean the hen, place the other ingredients inside and sew up. Simmer in water till cooked, then eat the flesh and drink the soup. Do this 3-10 times.

6. SCALDS. During the summer season the pith and seeds of the pumpkin should be placed in a jar and left for a long time. This can be applied to scalds.

CAUTION. *Feverish, sluggish people should avoid this vegetable.*

LOOFAH

TOWEL GOURD, SILK MELON

Luffa cylindrica (L.) M.J. Roem.

SI GUA

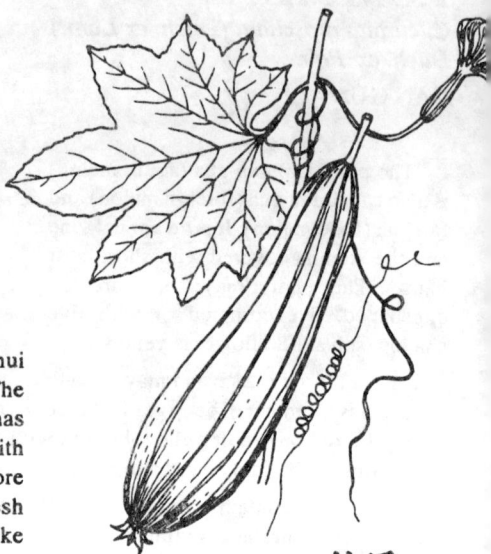

丝瓜

The loofah, si gua (silk melon), is also called shui gua (water melon). It is an annual climbing vine. The leaf is triangular or nearly circular and usually has 5-7 lobes. The fruit is long and cylindrical with troughs or grooves running along its length. Before it becomes fully ripe the fruit contains an edible flesh but as it ripens and dries this turns to a net-like filament. The seed is black, flat and with a fringe on the side.

The solid flesh, the so-called netting (loofah) and the vine are all used in medicine. The melon contains saponin, amaroid citrulline, xylan, protein, fat, sugar, calcium, phosphorous, iron, carotene, vitamins B1, B2, C, etc. The loofah netting contains xylan and fibre. The vine contains saponin.

The melon flavour is sweet, its nature cool, and it affects the heart, liver, lungs and stomach. The flavour of the loofah is sweet, its nature neither warm nor cool. The melon can cool fever, transform phlegm, cool the blood and neutralize poison. The loofah can stimulate the menstrual flow, cool fever and transform phlegm.

APPLICATIONS

1. INSUFFICIENT BREAST MILK SUPPLY. Take a piece of melon and some seeds. Dry by the fire till crisp, then crush to a powder. At regular periods take 3-6 grams of the powder in wine.

2. UTERINE BLEEDING. Take 1-2 strips of loofah, dry by the fire till crisp and grind to a powder and add a little brown sugar. Add to hot water and take in two serves.

3. LUMBAGO. Take a loofah and cut to pieces, bake over a slow fire till scorched yellow, then crush to a powder. Twice a day take 3 grams in wine.

4. CHRONIC BRONCHITIS. Take 100 grams of melon vine, simmer in water and serve. Continue this for three weeks.

5. MIGRAINE. Take 100 grams of the fresh roots of the melon and 2 duck eggs. Simmer in water and serve, eating the eggs and drinking the soup.

NOTES. *The silk melon and the Guandong silk melon, yue si gua, are not the same. The latter fruit is long and thin and has sharp ridges, however the medicinal effects are more or less the same. The former is often called shui gua (water melon, not to be confused with the western watermelon) and the latter Guandong silk melon or 8 angled silk melon.*

CUCUMBER
Cucumis sativus L.
HUANG GUA

The cucumber, huang gua (yellow melon), is also called hu gua (foreign melon). It is an annual creeping or climbing vine. It has a heart shaped leaf with 3-7 shallow lobes. The flower is yellow. The melon is cylindrical and the surface covered with small lumps. When ripe it is yellow-green. The seed is white and oval.

黄瓜

The melon, root, stem and leaf are all used in medicine. The melon contains protein, fat, sugar, calcium, phosphorous, iron, carotene, vitamins B1, B2, C, niacin, coffee acid, a variety of amino acids, volatile oils, etc.

The flavour of the melon is sweet, its nature cool, and it affects the spleen, stomach and large intestine. The melon can cool fever and benefit the urine. The vine can cool fever, benefit body moisture, dispel excessive phlegm and calm convulsions.

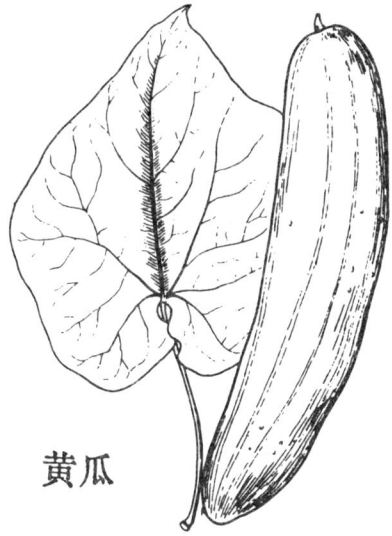

APPLICATIONS

1. DYSENTERY IN SMALL CHILDREN. Take an appropriate quantity of soft cucumber, slice and pickle in honey. Serve a little of this at regular intervals.

2. ACUTE THROAT INFLAMATION; TONSILLITIS. Take a little of the frosting (see the notes below), add crushed borneol; camphol (Borneolum Syntheticum) and blow into the throat.

3. SCALDING DIARRHOEA IN SMALL CHILDREN. Take some cucumber leaves, wash clean and crush to obtain the juice. Pour on hot water, add a little sugar and serve.

4. HIGH BLOOD PRESSURE. Take 150 grams of the vine, simmer in water and drink in place of tea.

5. IMPETIGO. Take some of the vine and bake in a slow heat till dry. Add an appropriate amount of alum and crush to a dust. Sprinkle this on the sores.

CAUTION: *People suffering from a cold empty feeling in the stomach should avoid this vegetable.*

NOTES: TO MAKE CUCUMBER FROSTING

(1) Select a ripe yellow melon, one that shows obvious lumps on the skin. Cut off the top and remove the pulp. Place some Glauber's salt in the melon, replace the top and fix it in place with toothpicks. Hang it up under the eaves of the house, but not in a place where it will get continuous sunshine. After a time frosting will appear on the skin and this can be scraped off for use.

(2) Another method is to open the melon, remove the pulp and add white alum. Tie the melon together again and hang in a cool, shady place that is well ventilated. When the frosting appears, scrape it off.

ORIENTAL PICKLING MELON
CHINESE WHITE CUCUMBER
Cucumis melo L. var. conomon (Thunb.) Makino

BAI GUA

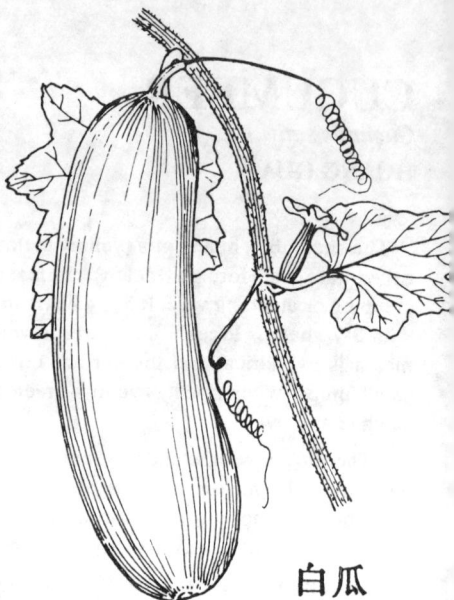

The oriental pickling melon, bai gua (white melon), is also called shao gua (top melon), cai gua (vegetable melon), yue gua (jump/exceed melon), sheng gua (live melon) and cha gua (tea melon). It is an annual creeping vine. The stem has thorn like hairs. The leaf is roughly circular or slightly kidney shaped with 3-7 shallow lobes.

白瓜

The fruit is cylindrical or club shaped, the outer surface bare and smooth with a number of shallow grooves on it. It is pale green or greenish white, the flesh is white, crisp and juicy. The seeds are white. The fruit is used in medicine. The nutritional value of the white melon and the yellow melon (cucumber) are roughly the same. The flavour is sweet, its nature cool, and it affects the intestines and stomach. It can benefit the urine and relieve alcoholic poisoning.

(This is the same family as the canteloupe or musk melon.)

APPLICATIONS

1. DIZZINESS AFTER DRINKING ALCOHOL; SUFFOCATING FEELING IN THE CHEST. Take a melon, wash clean, slice and pickle in vinegar. Take a serve of this.

2. FEVER AND THIRST. Take a quantity of melon, simmer in water, add sugar and drink in place of tea.

3. DIFFICULTY IN URINATING. Take some melon, wash clean and eat raw.

4. SORES IN THE CORNER OF THE MOUTH. Bake a melon until it turns to charcoal, then grind it to a powder. Add a little honey and apply this to the affected parts several times a day.

CAUTION. *People suffering from a cold empty feeling in the stomach should avoid this vegetable.*

BITTER MELON
BALSAM-PEAR
Momordica charantica L.
KU GUA

The bitter melon, ku gua (bitter melon), is also called lai gua (referring to the shape) and liang gua (cool melon). It is an annual climbing vine, the leaves shaped like a hand with 5-7 deep lobes. The flower is small and yellow, not longer than 20mm. The fruit is spindle shaped and covered in small lumps and knobs, and becomes yellow-orange when ripe, its flavour is bitter. The pulp is a bright red colour with a bitter-sweet flavour. Both fruit and plant are used in medicine.

The bitter melon contains protein, fat, calcium, phosphorous, iron, carotene, vitamins B1, B2, C, bitter melon glucoside, glutamic acid, alanine, proline, citrulline, pectin, etc. Its flavour is bitter, its nature cool and it affects heart, liver and lungs. It can relieve heat stroke, brighten the eye and neutralize poison.

苦瓜

APPLICATIONS
1. COMMON COLD WITH FEVER DURING HOT WEATHER; BODY PAINS AND BITTER TASTE IN THE MOUTH DURING SUMMER. Take 15 grams of dry bitter melon, 10 grams of spring onion and 6 grams of fresh ginger. Simmer in water and serve.

2. HEAT STROKE; SUNSTROKE. Take a bitter melon and discard the pith, then slice. Take 6 grams of tea leaves, simmer together in water and serve.

3. HOT, FLUSHED FEELING WITH THIRST. Take a bitter melon, discard the pith, slice, simmer in water and serve.

4. STOMACH ACHE. Roast a bitter melon to charcoal, then grind into a powder. For each serve take 1 gram in hot water, 2-3 times a day.

5. DYSENTERY. Take a fresh bitter melon and crush to obtain the juice, add hot water and serve. Another method is to sun dry the melon vine and grind it to a powder. For each serve add 3 grams to hot water and take at intervals of 6 hours.

6. ACUTE CONTAGIOUS CONJUNCTIVITIS. Take 15 grams of dried bitter melon and 10 grams of chrysanthemum flowers, simmer in water and serve.

7. BOIL, FURUNCLE. Take leaves of the melon, dry in the sun and grind into a powder. At regular intervals put 10 grams in wine and serve.

8. SWOLLEN BOILS AND CARBUNCLES. Crush the bitter melon to a paste and

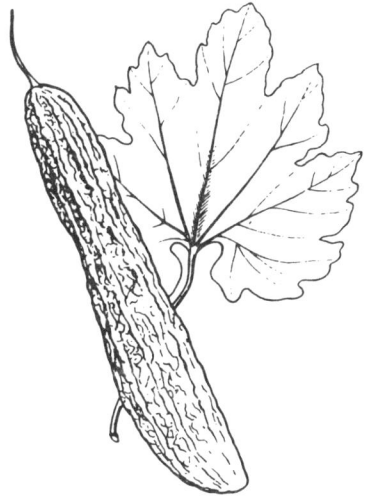

apply to the affected parts as a dressing.

CAUTION: *Persons suffering from a cold empty feeling in the stomach and spleen should avoid this melon.*

BOTTLE GOURD
CALABASH
Lagenaria siceraria (Molina) Standl.
HU LU

The bottle gourd, hu lu, is also called hu (gourd) and piao zi (gourd ladle). It is an annual climbing vine and is covered with sticky flexible hairs. The leaf is heart shaped and round with a slightly irregular outer edge or a few shallow lobes. The ends of the leaf stem show two lumps. The flower is white.

The fruit is large and has a distinct bottle gourd shape, with a large swelling at the bottom, a narrow waist and a smaller swelling above this. Within this shape there is a lot of variation, in some the upper part is like a bent neck, in others the melon looks like a dumbbell.

葫芦

When the fruit becomes ripe the skin hardens to a wood-like quality. The seeds are white. The flesh, skin and seeds are used in medicine. The fruit contains protein, fat, sugar, calcium, phosphorous, iron, carotene, vitamins B1, B2, C, etc. The flavour is sweet but insipid, its nature cool and it affects the lungs, spleen and kidneys. It can cool fever, promote diuresis and cleanse the urine.

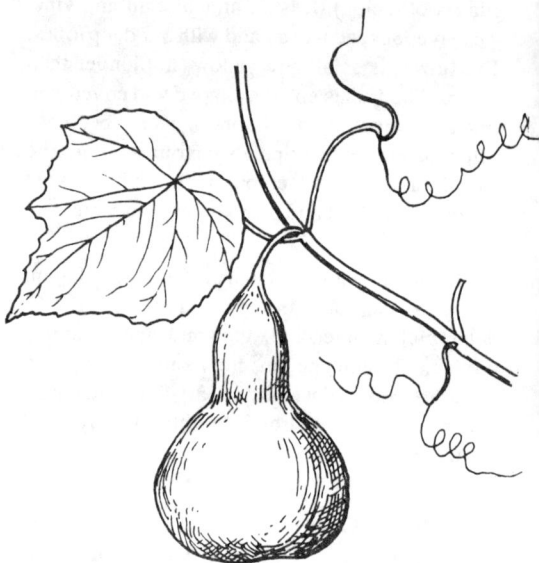

APPLICATIONS

1. ACUTE NEPHRITIS WITH DROPSY. Take 15-30 grams of dried gourd skin, simmer in water and serve. Another method is to take some old skin and bake over a slow fire till yellow, then grind to a powder. 2-3 times a day add 10 grams to boiled water and serve.

2. CIRRHOSIS WITH ASCITES. Take 15-30 grams of old shell, 60 grams of yellow soya beans, 15 grams of garlic and the head of a carp. Add water and simmer till the beans are cooked, then mash and serve.

EGGPLANT
AUBERGINE
Solanum melongena L.
JIA

The eggplant, jia, is also called jia gua (eggplant melon), qie zi (eggplant seed/suffix) and ai gua (short melon). It is a shrub that stands vertically with a number of branches. The leaf is large, irregular and roughly oval or egg shaped. The flower is large and white or mauve. The fruit may be long or round and white, red, deep purple, etc. The fruit, stem and leaves are used in medicine.

The eggplant contains protein, fat, sugar, calcium, phosphorous, iron, carotene, vitamins B1, B2, C, niacin and alkaloids. The skin contains a pigment glucoside and perilla glucoside. The flavour of the fruit is sweet-astringent, its nature cool, and it affects spleen, stomach and large intestine. The flavour of the root is bitter-sweet, its nature neither warm nor cool and it can benefit the stomach and large intestine. The fruit can cool fever, nourish the blood, ease pain and diminish swelling.

APPLICATIONS.

1. BLOOD IN THE FAECES. Take an eggfruit, including the stalk, and roast to charcoal, then grind to a powder. Twice a day add 3 grams to warm wine and serve. Another method is to take the leaves, dry them above the fire then crush to powder. For each serve add 6 grams to boiled salted water.

2. WHOOPING COUGH. Take 30 grams of old eggplant, discard the seeds, add a little brown sugar, simmer in water and serve.

3. CHRONIC RHEUMATISM AND ARTHRITIS. Take 15 grams of the root of the eggplant, simmer in water and serve. Another method is to take 100 grams of the root and soak it in 500 grams of white wine (sake may be used. Ed.) for a week. Twice a day serve 25 mls.

4. CHRONIC TRACHEITIS. Obtain a syrup made from eggplant roots and sugar. Two or three times a day take 50 mls.

5. SILVER RING SNAKE (*Bungarus muticinctus*) **BITE.** Boil the whole plant in water and make the affected person drink a large quantity within two hours of being bitten. At the same time get the patient to hospital as quickly as possible.

6. HOT AND PAINFUL INFECTED, SWOLLEN SORES. Crush eggplant and apply to the affected parts.

7. TINEA VERSICOLOR. Cut open an eggplant, dip in sulphur powder and apply to the affected place.

8. CHILBAINS. Take some of the whole plant, simmer in water and use the liquid to wash the affected parts.

CAUTION: *Persons with a persistent cough and a cold feeling in the lungs should avoid this vegetable.*

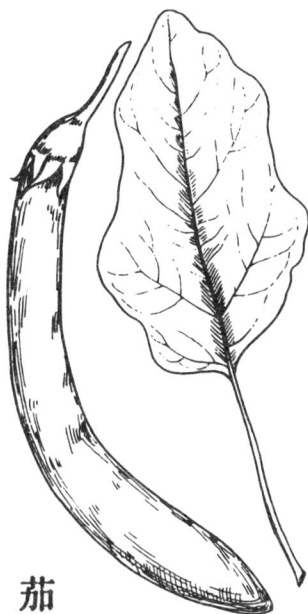

TOMATO

Lycopersicum esculentum Mill.
FAN QIE

番茄

The tomato, fan gie (foreign eggplant) is also called xi hong shi (western red persimmon), jin qian ju (golden coin tangerine) and fan shi (foreign persimmon).

Some varieties are annuals, others live for many years. The plant is covered by fine slightly sticky hairs. The plant carries feathery compound leaves or feathery leaves with deep splits. The flower is yellow. The berry may be like a flattened ball or round, and varies in colour from a fresh red to orange or yellow. The fruit and complete plant are used in medicine.

Tomatoes contains malic acid, citric acid, as well as a small amount of tomato alkali, protein, fat, sugar, calcium, phosphorous, iron, carotene, vitamins B1, B2 and C, niacin etc.

The flavour of the fruit is sweet and acidic, its nature neither hot nor cold and it is good for the stomach. It helps promote the secretion of saliva, quenches thirst, helps promote a healthy stomach and aids digestion.

APPLICATIONS

1. DIABETES. Take an equal quantity of tomato juice and watermelon juice, mix and drink at regular intervals. Another treatment is to take equal parts of tomato and pork pancreas, add a little oil and salt for flavour and boil into a soup. Drink this at regular intervals.

2. BLEEDING GUMS; GINGIVITIS. Wash a tomato clean and eat it. Eat at least a tomato daily for about a month.

3. ULCERS IN THE MOUTH. Cook together equal quantities of tomatoes and fresh fish and eat. Do this daily for one or two weeks until an improvement is noticed.

4. GASTRIC ULCER. Take one tomato and a pickled lemon and slice, add some honey and mix together. Take a small amount several times a day and continue this for three weeks.

5. SKIN, SWOLLEN AND POISONED. Take the whole stem of the tomato, including the leaves. Simmer in water and wash the affected parts.

CAUTION: *Persons suffering from hot, moist stomach and intestines should eat only small amounts of tomato.*

PAWPAW
PAPAYA
Carica papaya L.
FAN MU GUA

The pawpaw, fan mu gua (foreign tree melon) is also called wan shou guo (long life fruit), mu gua (tree melon) and fan gua (foreign melon).

The tree is of a soft nature and can grow as high as 8 metres (but is generally around 3 metres). The tree contains a milky sap. The lower part of the trunk usually has no branches, the leaves occuring at the top of the tree.

The leaf is shaped like the palm of a hand, with 7-9 deep splits in it. It carries a number of flowers on single stems of a cream or yellow colour.

The ripe fruit is orange or yellow, with thick flesh and black seeds in the centre. Both fruit and leaves are used in medicine.

番木瓜

The fruit contains papaya protease, rennin, carotene, protein, fat, glucose, fructose, sucrose, calcium, phosphorous, iron, tartaric acid, citric acid, malic acid, vitamins B1, B2 and C, etc.

The fruit flavour is sweet, its nature neither warm nor cool. It is useful in treating stomach and intestines. Its virtues are that it can aid digestion, tone the stomach, improve the flow of breast milk in nursing mothers, stimulate the circulation of the blood and relax joints and muscles.

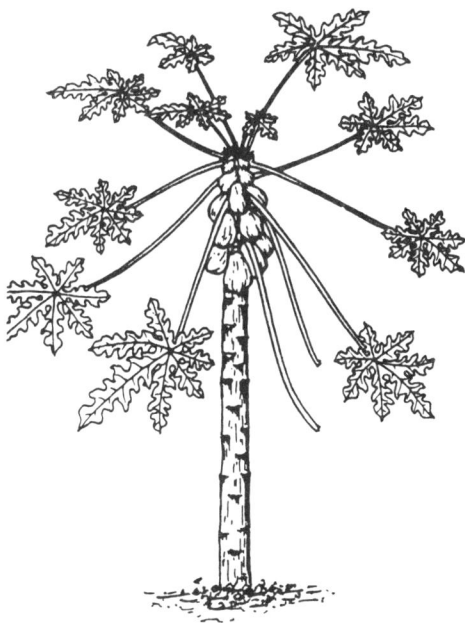

APPLICATIONS

1. INSUFFICIENT BREAST MILK. Take 500 grams of pawpaw and a pig's trotter. Simmer together into a soup and drink.

2. STOMACH ULCER; DUODENAL ULCER; PEPTIC ULCER. Eat ripe pawpaw at regular intervals.

3. RENAL COLIC, KIDNEY STONES, GALL STONES. Take 30 grams of male pawpaw flowers, simmer with 15 grams of lard into a soup and drink.

4. NAUSEA AND VOMITING DURING PREGNANCY. Roast pawpaw leaves till they turn to charcoal and crush to a fine dust. Dissolve 3 grams in a glass of water and drink 2-3 times a day.

5. ATHLETE'S FOOT. Take one large pawpaw leaf, 10 pomelo leaves, 30 grams of da feng gai (*Blumea balsamifera*) and 30 grams of Lu Ying (*Sambucus chinensis Lindl.*). Simmer in water and use the liquid to wash the affected part at frequent intervals.

6. ACHING MUSCLES; STIFF JOINTS. Take a ripe pawpaw and slice off the base of the fruit so that the seeds can be scooped out and discarded. Fill the cavity with rice wine (sake may be used) and replace the base, fixing it firmly in position with toothpicks. Place the fruit carefully in warm water and simmer it very gently for one hour. Pour the wine out into a bottle. Take 20-30 mls twice daily.

CHINESE OLIVE
Canarium album (Lour.) Raeusch.
LAN CHI

Lan chi is also called lan jiao (lan horn). It is a tall tree which can grow to 20 metres. The fruit is egg or oval shaped and 20-30mm in length, with both ends tapering. When ripe it is purple-black. Both the fruit and the fruit stone are used in medicine. The flavour of the fruit is astringent, its nature warm and it affects the liver and the large intestine. The flavour of the fruit stone is insipid, its nature neither warm nor cold. It helps liven a sluggish nature.

橄豉

APPLICATIONS
1. AFTER RECOVERY FROM MEASLES THE CHILD HAS NO APPETITE AND SUFFERS FROM DYSENTERY. Take 6 fruit and an appropriate quantity of rice and boil into a gruel. Eat this twice a day for 2 or 3 days.

2. FISHBONE STUCK IN THE THROAT. Grind some fruit stones with vinegar and hold this in the mouth and throat for as long as possible. Another treatment is to roast the fruit stones to charcoal and crush to a fine powder. Blow this into the throat one or two times.

WARNING: *People suffering from hot stomach pains should eat only small quantities of this fruit.*

PEA
Pisum sativum L.
WAN DOU

The pea, wan dou, is also called he lan dou (Dutch bean) and xue dou (snow bean). It is an annual, and a climbing plant. The pod is roughly rectangular and 50-80mm long. The inside of the pod has a thin paper like lining. The seeds are round and green, changing to yellow when dry. The seeds are used in medicine.

They contain protein, fat, sugar, phosphorous, iron, carotene, vitamins, B1, B2 and C, niacin, gibberellin etc. The flavour is sweet and the nature of the seeds neither warm nor cool. They are beneficial to spleen and stomach, encourage secretion of saliva and stop thirst.

豌豆

APPLICATIONS

1. TO DIMINISH THIRST. Take an appropriate quantity of peas, lightly boil and eat frequently without salt.

2. LACK OF ENERGY. Take an appropriate quantity of peas and mutton, simmer and eat.

3. HEATSTROKE WITH VOMITING AND DIARRHOEA. Take 60 grams of peas and 10 grams of Chinese mosla (*Mosla chinensis*). Simmer in water and serve.

4. LACK OF MILK JUST BEFORE AND AFTER BIRTH. Take 250 grams of peas and one pig's trotter, simmer in water and serve.

5. CHLOASMA, BROWN BLOTCHY DICOLOURATION ON THE FACE. Simmer a quantity of peas in water and wash the affected parts with the liquid. Do this frequently until results can be seen.

COWPEA
BLACK-EYED PEA

Vigna unguiculata (L.) Walp. subsp. sesquipedalis (l.) Verdc.

DOU JIAO

The cowpea, dou jiao (bean horn), is also called jiang dou (cowpea). An annual twining plant, it has small egg-shaped leaves arranged in groups of three. The flowers form in groups of 3-6, the corolla a pale mauve colour.

The pod is narrow, 200-400mm long and hangs from the plant. It is flexible and contains kidney shaped seeds. Seeds, leaves and root are all used in medicine.

The seed contains a large amount of starch and also fat, protein, niacin, vitamins B1, B2 and C, sugar, calcium, phosphorous, iron and carotene. 豆角

The flavour of the seed is sweet and astringent, its nature neither warm nor cool. It is beneficial to the spleen and stomach.

The seed invigorates the spleen and nourishes the kidneys. The leaf cools a fever and benefits the urine, while the root invigorates the spleen and aids digestion.

APPLICATION

1. NOT MAKING SUFFICIENT URINE. Take 120 grams of cowpea leaves, simmer in water, add a little brown sugar and serve.

2. MALNUTRITION IN SMALL CHILDREN DUE TO DIGESTIVE PROBLEMS. Dry the root of the cowpea in the sun and grind into a powder. At regular intervals mix 10 grams with a cooked hen egg or steamed lean pork and eat.

3. DROPSY CAUSED BY POOR NUTRITION. Take 250 grams of cowpeas and an appropriate quantity of pork bones. Cook into a soup, eat the cowpeas and drink the soup.

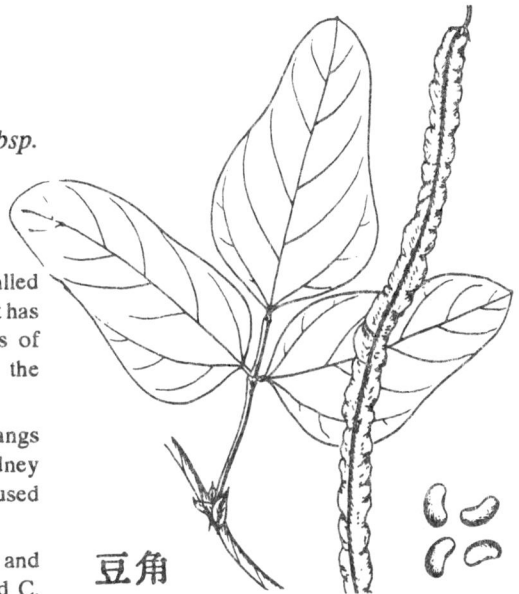

SWORD BEAN
Canavalia gladiata (Jacq.) DC.
DAO DOU

刀豆

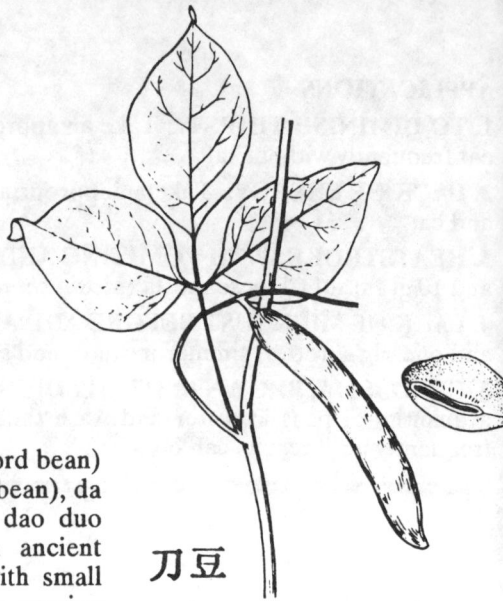

The sword bean, dao dou (knife/sword bean) is also called xie jian dou (short sword bean), da dao du (great knife bean) and guan dao duo (Guan's sword bean. Guan was an ancient Chinese hero). It is a twining vine with small leaves in clusters of three, the ends coming gradually to a point and the base part rounded, the texture thin.

The flower is pink or mauve. The pod is shaped like a knife and 200-350mm long, with a bulging ridge along the edge. The seed is oval or kidney shaped and red or brown, it has a "navel" about 3/4 of its length. The seed, root and pod shell all are used in medicine.

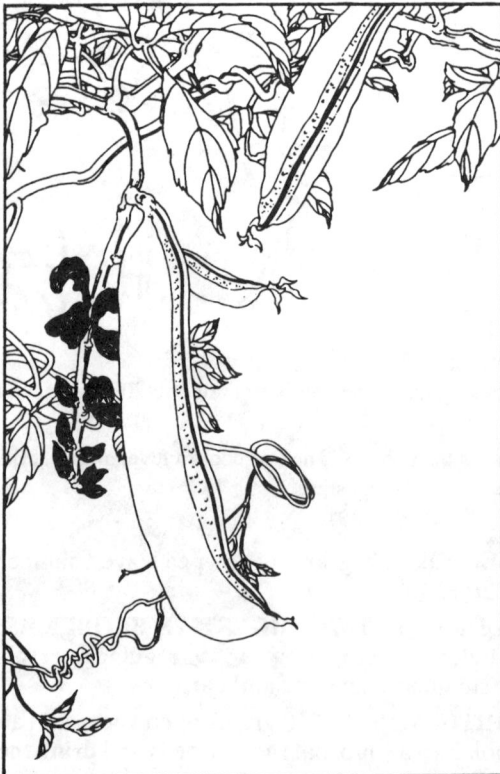

The seed contains urea, sword bean animo acid, starch, protein, fat, calcium, phosphorous, iron, carotene, Vitamin C, etc. The flavour of the seed is sweet-astringent, its nature warm. It affects the stomach, liver and kidneys. The shell of the bean has a sweet-astringent flavour, its nature neither warm nor cool. It affects the liver and stomach. The root has a bitter flavour and a warm nature, it affects the liver and kidneys.

The seed can warm the stomach and nourish the kidneys. The shell clears the blood and helps stop diarrohea. The root clears the blood and helps ease pain.

APPLICATIONS
1. LUMBAGO WITH KIDNEY PAINS. Take two seeds, simmer till cooked and chew with a little wine. Do this twice

a day. Another treatment is to take 30 grams of the roots, simmer in water and discard the sediment. Mix with an appropriate amount of glutinous rice, cook and serve. Do this once a day.

2. LUMBAGO IN PREGNANT WOMAN. Take 60 grams of sword bean shells and a hen egg. Simmer both in water then eat the egg and drink the soup.

3. RHEUMATISM AND LUMBAGO. Take 30 grams of sword bean root and simmer it in an equal quantity of wine and water, then serve.

4. HERNIA IN SMALL CHILDREN. Dry sword bean seeds in the sun and grind into a powder. Every day mix 5 grams in water and drink.

5. VOMITING AFTER EATING: DIFFICULTY IN SWALLOWING. Take 15 grams of sword bean shell, 3 pieces of salted Chinese olive (*Canarium Album*) stones and 10 grams of *Pinellia ternata (Thunb.) Breit.*. Simmer in water and serve.

6. HICCUPS. Roast sword bean shells into charcoal and crush to dust. Put 5-10 grams into warm water and sip at regular intervals.

7. AMENORRHOEA IN PREGNANT WOMEN: STOMACH SWOLLEN AND PAINFUL. Take sword bean shells, roast dry and crush into dust. Put 3 grams into yellow wine and drink twice a day.

8. BREAST PAIN IN WOMEN. Take an equal amount of sword beans and the fibres of a loofah. Roast to charcoal and crush into dust. Twice a day mix 10 grams in yellow wine and drink.

CAUTION: People with a feverish stomach should be cautious in eating this bean.

Editor's Note. *Sword or Madagascar beans can cause a bad stomachache if not eaten young, this has been our experience. Although they are a delicious bean we no longer grow them for this reason. Herklots p.233 suggests boiling them in two changes of salted water and eating only a few on the first occasion. If there are no side effects then more can be eaten at future meals.*

BROAD BEAN
Vicia faba L.
CAN DOU

The broad bean, can cou (silkworm bean) is also called hu dou (foreign bean), ma chi dou (horse tooth bean), nan dou (south bean) and luo fan dou (net float bean). It is an annual with a vertical stem. The small leaf is oval. The flower is white, shading to pink with mauve stripes.

The pod is 40-80mm long and thick. The seed is oval and slightly flat, when ripe it is green-brown or red-brown in colour. The stem, flower, pod, seed skin, seed and leaf are all used in medicine.

Broad beans contain protein, fat, sugar, calcium, phosphorous, iron, carotene, vitamins B1, B2, C, niacin, phospholipid, choline, etc. The flavour of the broad bean is sweet, its nature neither warm nor cool. It affects the spleen and stomach.

蚕豆

The bean can invigorate the spleen, benefit secretion of moisture, calm the stomach and stop diarrhoea. The stem can stop bleeding and prevent diarrhoea. The leaf is astringent and can help stop bleeding. The flower cools the blood and can help stop bleeding. The skin of the seed benefits the urine and prevents involuntary urination. The pod is astringent and can help stop bleeding.

APPLICATIONS

1. CHOKING WITH NAUSEA; VOMITING. Take some dry broad beans and grind into powder. Place 10 grams in hot water with a little brown sugar and serve. Do this two or three times a day.

2. PUFFINESS OF THE FLESH. Take 250 grams of broad beans, 30 grams of garlic and an appropriate measure of brown sugar. Simmer in water and serve.

3. OEDEMA, DROPSY. Take 60 grams of broad beans and 15 grams of pumpkin or winter melon skin. Simmer together in water and serve.

4. TUBERCULOSIS WITH COUGHING OF BLOOD. Take a quantity of leaves of the broad bean, crush and obtain the juice. Take 20mls twice a day.

5. CONTINUING FEELING OF INTOXICATION AFTER DRINKING; DRUNKEN PERSON NOT WAKING. Take an appropriate quantity of broad bean sprouts, add oil, salt and water and boil into a soup and make the patient drink.

6. VARIOUS TYPES OF INTERNAL HAEMORRHAGE. Take some broad bean stems and bake dry, then crush into a powder. Add 6 grams to some warm water and drink. Do this three times a day.

7. HIGH BLOOD PRESSURE. Take 10 grams of broad bean flowers and 15 grams of the beard of maize or corn. Simmer together in water and serve.

8. HOT COUGH WITH COUGHING UP BLOOD. Take 10 grams of broad bean flowers and simmer in water. Discard the sediment and dissolve some crystal sugar in the remaining liquid. Drink a measure of this twice a day.

9. URINE BLOCKAGE. Take 100 grams of broad bean shells, simmer in water and eat at frequent intervals.

10. WATERY DIARRHOEA. Take 30 grams of broad bean stems, simmer in water and serve.

11. LEG ULCERS THAT WILL NOT HEAL. Mash leaves of the broad bean and apply to the affected places.

12. PEMPHIGUS; SCALDS. Take some broad bean pods and stir fry until they become charcoal. Crush into a powder, mix with a little sesame oil and apply to the affected place.

CAUTION: *A very small number of people, mainly male children, have an allergy to the broad bean as food or to the pollen of the flowers, and this can result in haemolysis type anaemia, commonly called can dou huang bing (broad bean yellow illness). This should be kept in mind.*

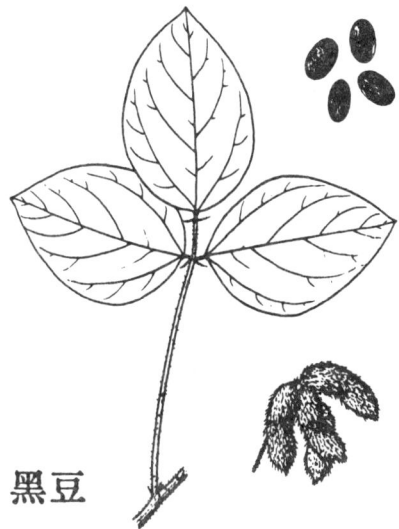

BLACK SOYBEAN
Glycine soja Sieb. et Zucc.
HEI DOU

(The black soybean and the yellow soybean are the two most popular varieties of soybeans grown in China. According to Herklots p.241 the black soybean contains more protein than the yellow variety, while the yellow variety has more fat or oil than the black. Ed)

The black soybean, hei dou (black bean), is also called wu dou (black bean) and hei da dou (black great bean). It is an annual with a thick stem. The leaves are in groups of three and have hairs on both sides. The flowers are white or pale mauve.

黑豆

The pod is of a rectangular shape, slightly bent and yellow green in colour, covered with long stiff hairs. The seed is egg shaped or close to ball shape. The seed may be cream colour or black, it is the latter which is known as the black bean. Both the seed and the seed skin are used in medicine.

The bean contains an abundant amount of protein as well as fat, carbohydrate, calcium, phosphorous, iron, carotene, vitamins B1, B2 and niacin etc. The flavour of the bean is sweet and slightly astringent, its nature neither warm nor cool. It acts on liver and kidneys.

The flavour of the skin seed is sweet, its nature cool. It affects the liver.

The black soy bean helps correct a deficiency of yin, nourishes the blood, calms the spirit, brightens the eye and benefits the kidneys. The seed skin nourishes the blood and disperses wind.

APPLICATIONS
1. KIDNEY AND WAIST PAINS. Take 100 grams of black soybeans, a tang jiao fish (clarias fuscus L.) and 10 grams of the bark of eucommia (*Eucommia ulmoides*). Add water and simmer till the beans are cooked. Discard the bark, add a little peanut oil

and salt for flavour and mix together. Divide into two and serve in the course of a day.

2. DEFICIENCY OF YIN IN SMALL CHILDREN RESULTING IN A FEVER. Take 10 grams each of black soybeans, yellow soybeans and mung beans. Simmer in water and serve.

3. BED-WETTING IN SMALL CHILDREN, ENURESIS. Take 500 grams of black soybeans and soak in the urine of a boy under the age of 12 until the bean skins begin to wrinkle. Remove the beans and stir fry them until they are cooked. Chew 10 grams of the beans two or three times a day and wash down with slightly salty water.

4. INFANT HOT AND UPSET. Take 10 grams of black soybeans, 3 grams of licorice root, about half a gram of rushes and 10 grams of young pale bamboo leaves. Simmer in water and serve.

5. BERIBERI. Take an appropriate measure of equal quantities of black soybeans and Chinese white rice beans. Add water and simmer till reduced to a thick juice. Drink one small cup of this 2-3 times a day for 5-7 days.

6. ANEMIA WITH DROPSY. Take 100 grams of black soybeans, add 500 mls of water and simmer till it is reduced to 200mls. Add 100mls of sweet wine and again simmer for 10 minutes. Take twice a day.

7. DIFFICULTY IN PASSING OF URINE BY SMALL CHILDREN. Take 120 black soybeans and crush them. Add 2 grams of licorice root and water and simmer until there is about 100 mls of liquid. Mix in 3 grams of pure talc and drink all at once.

8. KIDNEY ASTHENIA DUE TO DIABETES. Stir fry an equal quantity of black soybeans and the root of Chinese trichosanthes (*Trichosanthes kirilowii*). Crush into a fine powder, add a small amount of honey and roll into pills about the size of a black bean or a little larger. At each serve add 70 of these pills to black soybean soup or to slightly salted water. Serve twice daily.

9. METRORRHAGIA. Take 250 grams of black soybeans and 500 mls of rice wine. First stir fry the beans until they just begin to smoke. Remove from the flames and pour on the wine while the beans still retain their heat. The wine will turn a reddish-purple colour. Take 15-30mls of this mixture three times a day.

10. LUMBAGO DURING PREGNANCY. Take 100 grams of black soybeans and 300 mls of sweet wine. Simmer together and serve.

YELLOW SOYBEAN
SOYA BEAN

Glycine max (l.) Merr.
HUANG DOU

The yellow soybean, huang duo (yellow bean) is also called da dou (great bean). It is an annual with a rough stem. The leaf is small and grouped into three, both sides of the leaf are covered with white hairs. The flower is white or mauve.

The pod is roughly rectangular, slightly curved, yellow- green in colour and covered with long hard hairs. The seed is egg shaped or near ball shaped and the colour of the skin may be cream or black. The cream variety is called the yellow bean, the black variety is called the black bean.

黄豆

The seed is used in traditional medicine, it is very nutritious and contains protein, fat, carbohydrate, calcium, phosphorous, iron, vitamins B1 and B2 and niacin. The flavour is sweet and its nature is neither warm nor cool.

It affects the spleen and the large intestine. It is used to treat stomach complaints, to moisten the respiratory tract and diminish swelling.

APPLICATIONS

1. MALNUTRITION WITH DROPSY. Take 250 grams of yellow soybeans, add a litre of water and simmer until it has reduced to one quarter of the volume. Add an appropriate measure of sweet wine. Take this three times a day.

2. BERIBERI WITH DROPSY. Take 120 grams of yellow soybeans, 200 grams of garlic and some crystal sugar. Simmer together with water and serve three times a day.

3. CRAMPS IN HANDS AND FEET. Take 100 grams of yellow soybeans and 60 grams of rice bran. Add water and simmer till it becomes like porridge. Eat twice a day.

4. WATERY DIARRHOEA CAUSED BY DISORDER OF THE SPLEEN. Take 100 grams of yellow soybeans and 15 grams of the rhizome of *Atractylodes macrocephala*. Crush to a fine powder. Three times a day drink a small quantity of the water in which rice has been cooked, mixing 10 grams of the powder to each serve.

5. BURNS; SCALDS. Every day during the recovery period drink the liquid obtained by steaming yellow soybeans. This speeds up the healing time and reduces scars.

6. ERYSIPELAS IN SMALL CHILDREN. Simmer yellow soybeans in water till reduced to a thick liquid. Apply to the affected place.

7. EARLY STAGES IN A BOIL. Soak yellow soybeans in water till they have swollen up. Crush into a paste and spread on the affected parts and cover.

8. PULMONARY ABSCESS. Take 250 grams of yellow soybeans, wash clean and soak in cool boiled water until the water has penetrated the beans. Crush to obtain the juice, add a little sugar and drink it cool.

9. PRECAUTION AGAINST MEASLES. Take 30 grams of yellow soybeans and 30 grams of black soybeans. Add water and boil into a soup. Drinking this can prevent or alleviate the effects of measles.

CAUTION: *Persons recovering from small pox should not eat yellow soybeans or their byproducts.*

NOTES:

1. BEAN CURD.

Bean curd is made from soybeans. Its flavour is sweet and bland, its nature is cool. It affects the spleen, stomach and large intestine. It has a beneficial effect on the qi and internal organs, can increase the flow of saliva, clear fever and remove poison.

APPLICATIONS

1. COMMON COLD WITH DRY MOUTH AND BITTER TASTE IN THE MOUTH. Take 500 grams of bean curd, 250 grams of leaf mustard, 5 salted chinese olives and 10 grams of fresh ginger. Simmer together with water and serve.

2. COUGH WITH DRY MOUTH, DIFFICULTY IN COUGHING UP PHLEGM. Take one piece of bean curd and place it in a bowl. Dig a small hole in the centre about the size of a coin (25mm) and fill with sugar. Place the bowl in a container of water and gently simmer the water for one hour. Divide into two parts and eat in the course of a day.

3. TOOTHACHE. Take 500 grams of bean curd and 250 grams of leaf mustard. Add water and simmer for a long time. Add a little salt. Serve twice a day.

CAUTION: *People suffering from what the Chinese describe as a cold, empty feeling in the stomach and spleen should not eat bean curd.*

2. BEAN SPROUTS.

The soybean sprout is a tender and very nutritious green vegetable. The flavour is sweet and its nature cool. It has a beneficial effect upon the spleen and bladder. It moistens the system, clears feverish heat, aids in the retention of moisture and helps remove poison.

APPLICATIONS

1. RECOVERING FROM BLOOD LOSS OR POOR BLOOD. Take 250 grams of soybean shoots, 15 grams of Chinese dates (jujubes) and 250 grams of pork bones. Add water and simmer for a long time, blend in a little salt. Three times a day eat some of the bean shoots and drink the soup.

2. PULMONARY TUBERCULOSIS. Take 500 grams of soybean shoots and 250 grams of pork backbone. Simmer with water for a long time, blending in a little salt. Three times a day eat some of the shoots and drink the soup.

3. COMMON WART; FISH SCALE MOLE. Take an appropriate quantity of soybean shoots and boil with water into a clear soup. Drink this for three successive days as one course of treatment. During this time do not eat cereals or any oil or fats. On the fourth day go back to a normal diet, but continue to eat bean sprouts with rice.

4. EARLY STAGES OF CIRRHOSIS OF THE LIVER; ASCITES. Take 250 grams of soybean shoots and 250 grams of red beans (also known as rice beans *Phaseolus calcaratus*). Boil into a light soup and drink. Serve frequently to have an effect.

CAUTION: *If the flow of urine is consistently poor and weak avoid eating large quantities of bean shoots.*

RICE BEAN
A variety of COWPEA

*Vigna unguiculata (L.) Walp. subsp..
cylindrica (L.) Verde.*

FAN DOU

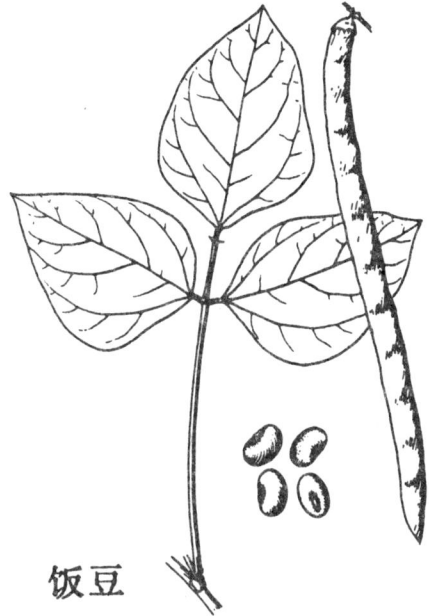

饭豆

The rice bean, fan dou, is also called mei dou (eyebrow bean), gan dou (sweet bean), bai dou (white bean) and fan jiang dou (rice cowpea). The leaves are grouped in threes and are roughly egg shaped. The flower is cream, tinged with mauve.

The pod is cylindrical, 70-130mm long. The seed is oval or kidney shaped, frequently cream in colour or dark red. The seed is used in medicine.

It contains protein, fat, carbohydrates, calcium, phosphorous, iron, vitamins B1 and B2 and niacin. The flavour is slightly astringent, its nature neither warm nor cool and it affects the spleen. It can invigorate the spleen and internal organs, promote diuresis and diminish swelling.

APPLICATIONS

1. POOR NUTRITION LEADING TO DROPSY. Take 120 grams of rice beans, 15 grams of garlic and an appropriate quantity of sugar. Simmer in water and serve.

2. BERIBERI LEADING TO DROPSY; FEELING OF NUMBNESS IN THE LIMBS; LACK OF STRENGTH. Take 200 grams of rice beans, 20 grams of red Chinese dates, 6 grams of dried orange skin and an appropriate amount of white or brown sugar. Simmer in water and serve.

MUNG BEAN
BLACK GRAM, GREEN GRAM
Vigna radiata (L.) Wilczek
LU DOU

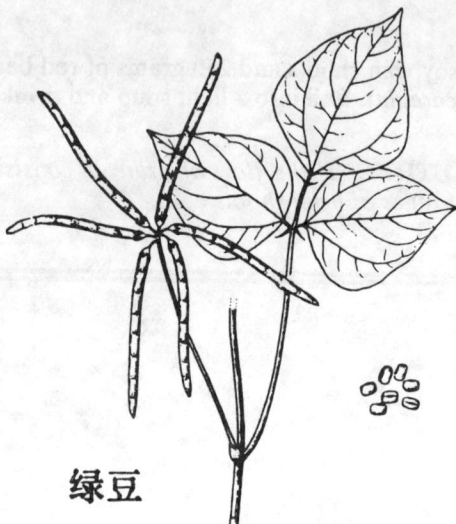

The mung bean, lu dou (green bean) is also called qing xiao dou (blue-green small bean). It is an annual vertical plant with smooth edged leaves in groups of three and has yellow flowers. The pod is cylindrical, 60-80mm long and covered with stiff hairs. The seeds are generally green, more rarely yellow-brown with a light patch on one end. Both seed and pod are used in medicine.

绿豆

The bean contains protein, fat, carbohydrate, calcium, phosphorous, iron, carotene, vitamins B1, B2 and niacin.

The bean sprout contains the same components plus vitamin C. However there is only a small measure of carotene.

The flavour of the bean and sprout is sweet-astringent, its nature cool and it affects the heart and stomach.

The mung bean can cool fever, neutralize poison, diminish heat stroke and help moisten the internal organs.

APPLICATIONS

1. HEATSTROKE. Take an appropriate quantity of mung beans, winter melon, kelp and lotus leaf, add water and boil into a soup. Add a little sugar or salt for flavour and serve.

2. CHICKEN POX IN SMALL CHILDREN. Take 10 grams of mung beans, 10 grams of red beans (also known as rice beans, adzuki beans, *Phaseolus calcaratus*), 10 grams of black soybeans and 3 grams of licorice root. Add water and simmer till the beans are cooked. Serve a small amount 2-3 times a day and continue this for a week.

3. CHRONIC THIRST. Take an appropriate quantity of mung beans and boil into a porridge. Eat this frequently.

4. CONSTANT HUNGRY FEELING EVEN AFTER EATING. Take equal quantities of mung bean, yellow wheat and glutinous rice and grind to a powder. Three times a day take 3 grams in boiled water.

5. MUMPS. Take 60 grams of mung beans, add water and simmer until partly cooked. Add 200 grams of the heart of Chinese cabbage (bai cai) and cook for 20 minutes. Once or twice a day serve this amount, including the liquid, and repeat for a number of days.

6. MEASLES WITH ENTERITIS IN SMALL CHILDREN. Take 15 grams of the outer covering of the mung bean, simmer in water, add a little sugar and serve.

7. ERYSIPELAS IN SMALL CHILDREN. Take equal quantities of mung beans and Chinese rhubarb, plus a little field mint or peppermint. Grind together into a paste, add a little honey and apply to the affected parts.

8. CHINESE MONKSHOOD (*Aconitum carmichaeli*) **POISONING; LEAD POISONING.** Take 120 grams of mung beans and 60 grams of licorice root. Add water, simmer and serve.

CAUTION: *Persons suffering with a cold empty feeling in the spleen and stomach should avoid mung beans.*

PEANUT
GROUNDNUT

Arachis hypogaea L.

HUA SHENG

花生

The peanut, hua sheng (flower live), is also called luo hua sheng (drop down flower live), di guo (earth fruit), chang sheng guo (long life earth fruit) and di duo (earth bean). It is an annual with multiple small leaves, usually in pairs and shaped like an inverted egg.

The flower is yellow. The pod is swollen and the outside covered with a net-like grain and contracted in the middle. The seed may be nearly round or oval and covered with a red or pale yellow skin. The seed, seed skin, shell, branches and leaves are all used in medicine.

The seed contains fat oil, protein, carbohydrates, calcium, phosphorous, iron, amino acids, lecithin, etc. The flavour of the seed is sweet, its nature neither warm nor cool and it affects the spleen and lungs. The flavour of the skin of the seed is slightly bitter and astringent. Its nature neither warm nor cool and it affects the lungs. The flavour of the shell is insipid and astringent, its nature neither warm nor cool and it affects the lungs. The flavour of the leaves and branches is bitter-sweet, their nature is cool and they affect the lungs.

The seed acts as a tonic on the spleen, moistens the lungs and nourishes the blood. The skin of the seed invigorates the spleen and stops bleeding. The shell acts on the lungs and helps stop coughing. The leaves and branches aid the liver and calm the nerves.

APPLICATIONS

1. DECREASING GLUTAMATIC PYRUVIC TRANSAMINASE (An enzyme found in the liver). Take 60 grams of peanuts, 30 grams of red Chinese dates and some crystal sugar. Simmer in water and serve.

2. HIGH BLOOD PRESSURE. Take 60 grams of the leaves and branches, simmer in water and serve. Another treatment is to take peanuts and soak them in vinegar. First thing in the morning, eat 10 pieces.

3. INSOMNIA. Take 60 grams of peanut leaves and branches, add water and simmer till reduced to 100 mls. Serve twice a day.

4. POOR NUTRITION ASSOCIATED WITH DROPSY. Take 60 grams of peanuts, a piece of crucian carp and 30 grams of red Chinese dates. Simmer in water, add peanut oil and salt for flavour and serve.

5. INADEQUATE SUPPLY OF BREAST MILK. Take 100 grams of peanuts and a front pig's trotter. Simmer together till cooked, add a little salt for flavour and serve.

6. BERIBERI. Take 60 grams of peanuts, 60 grams of rice beans and 30 grams of red Chinese dates. Simmer in water, add a little sugar and serve.

7 HIGH BLOOD FAT, HYPERLIPAEMIA. Take 30 grams of peanut shells and 30 grams of lotus leaves. Simmer in water and serve.

8. PURPURA; INTERNAL BLEEDING. Take 20 grams of the inner skin of the peanut and 30 grams of small red Chinese dates. Simmer in water and serve.

9. CHRONIC BRONCHITIS. Take 60 grams of the inner skin of the peanut, add water and simmer gently for about 10 hours then strain the liquid to get about 100 mls. Add a little sugar and take twice a day.

10. ASTHMA COUGH; SPITTING PHLEGM WITH BLOOD. Take 30 grams of peanut shells, 15 grams of loquat leaves and 15 grams of lily. Simmer in water and serve.

11. ROUND WORM CAUSING INTESTINAL OBSTRUCTION. Obtain fresh peanut oil. For children under the age of 15, serve 60 mls. For patients over 15, serve 80 mls. If there is no improvement after 6 hours, repeat the dose.

CAUTION: *Persons suffering from diarrhoea should avoid eating peanuts.*

FENNEL
Foeniculum vulgare Mill.
HUI XIANG

Fennel, hui xiang, is also called xiao hui xiang (small fennel) and bei hui xiang (north fennel). It may be an annual or live for a number of years. The foliage is pale green and has a characteristic smell. The leaves are feathery.

The flowers are small, in clusters, and yellow. The fruit is round or oval and yellow-green, with five vertical, angular bulges. The fruit, leaves and stem are used in medicine.

Fennel contains protein, fat, carbohydrate, calcium, phosphorous, iron, carotene, as well as a small amount of vitamins B1, B2, C, niacin, volatile oils (the principal ones being anethol, fenchone, anisic aldehyde and anisic acid).

The flavour of the plant is pungent, its nature warm, and it affects kidneys, liver and stomach. It can warm the kidney, disperse cold sensations, calm the stomach and regulate the flow of vital energy.

茴香

APPLICATIONS

1. INCARCERATED HERNIA OF THE SMALL INTESTINE. Take 10-15 grams of fennel (reduce the amount for small children) and crush. Pour on boiling water to make a soup and serve while still hot.

2. LIQUID ACCUMULATING UNDER THE SKIN OF THE TESTICLES; SWELLING OF THE TESTICLES. Take 15 grams of fennel and 5 grams of salt and stir fry until slightly scorched, then crush to a powder. Break in one or two green shelled duck eggs and cook into an omelette. Just before sleep serve this with warm rice wine. Do this for 4 days as one course of treatment. Repeat the treatment 2-5 days later if necessary.

3. SWELLING OF THE TESTICLES. Take 10 grams each of fennel and Siberian cockleburs (*Xanthium sibiricum*) and simmer in water. Take a small amount twice a day.

4. LUMBAGO DUE TO WEAK KIDNEYS. Take 10 grams of fennel and stir-fry till scorched yellow, then grind to a powder. Take a piece of belly pork and cut 10 slices into it, but not right through. Rub the fennel into the cuts, then wrap the pork in wet paper and cook. Chew the meat well and take a litle wine with it.

5. TO DIMINISH THIRST (The type of thirst causing excessive drinking followed by frequent urination during the night); POLYDIPSIA. Take 100 grams of fennel and a little salt, stir fry, then crush. Cook a bowl of glutinous rice, mix in the crushed fennel and eat.

6. COLD FEELING IN THE STOMACH WITH STOMACH ACHE; ABDOMINAL PAINS. Take 6 grams of fennel, 6 grams of galangal (*Alpinia officinarum*), 6 grams of three nerved spice-bush (*Lindera aggregata*), 10 grams of the rhizome of the nutgrass (*Cyperus rotundus*). Simmer in water and serve.

7. DIZZINESS WITH A TIGHT FEELING AROUND THE HEART, VOMITING CLEAR LIQUID. Take 250 grams of the stem and leaves of fennel, add a little peanut oil and salt for flavour, add water, boil into a soup and serve.

8. PAINFUL SWOLLEN BOILS; INFECTED ABSCESS. Take 500 grams of fennel, wash clean and crush to obtain the juice. Drink the juice and apply the sediment to the affected parts.

9. RHEUMATIC PAINS IN THE JOINTS. Take 30 grams of fennel root and 30 grams of tu fu ling (*Smilax glabra Roxb.*). Simmer in water and serve.

CAUTION: *Persons suffering a deficiency of yin should avoid this plant.*

DILL
Anethum graveolens. L
SHI LUO

Dill, shi luo (transplant plant) is also called tu hui xiang (earth fennel). It is an annual aromatic herb. It has feathery foliage and yellow flowers.

The fruit is oval with ridges running down its length. Fruit, leaf and stem are used in medicine.

The fruit contains carvone and dill-apiol. The stem and leaves contain vitamin C and a small amount of vitamin B2. The fruit has a pungent flavour, a warm nature and affects liver, kidneys and stomach. It can warm the kidneys, invigorate the stomach and disperse cold.

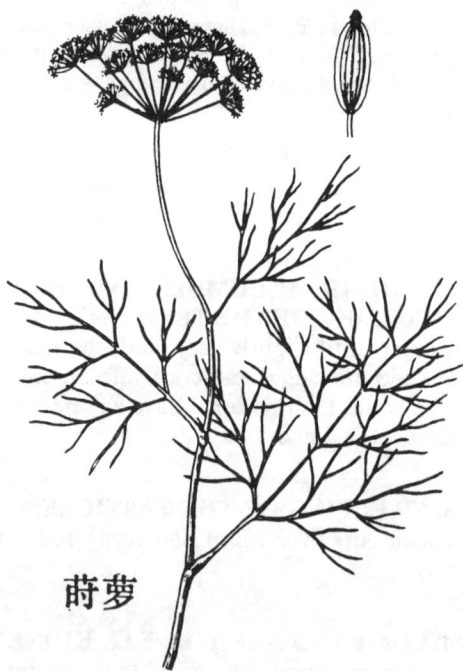

蒔蘿

APPLICATIONS

1. COUGHING AT NIGHT; EXCESSIVE WHITE FROTHY PHLEGM. Take an appropriate amount of dill fruit and 10 red Chinese dates. Remove the stones from the dates and stuff them with the dill. Place in water, add some crystal sugar and peanut oil and simmer till the dates are cooked then drink the soup and eat the dates.

2. COLD FEELING IN THE STOMACH WITH STOMACH ACHE IN SMALL CHILDREN. Take an appropriate quantity of dill fruit, pulverize and apply to the child's navel.

3. HERNIA OF THE TESTICLES; PAINFUL SWELLING IN THE LOWER ABDOMEN IN WOMEN. Take a quantity of dill fruit and stir-fry until they are roasted brown, then grind into a powder. At regular intervals take 10 grams of the powder in wine.

4. MUSCULAR STRAIN CAUSING LUMBAGO. Take a quantity of dill fruit and grind into a powder. At regular intervals take 10 grams in water.

5. EMPTY FEELING IN THE KIDNEYS WITH DIZZINESS AND HEADACHES. Take 250 grams of the leaves and stems of dill and one or two hen eggs or some lean pork, plus a little salt and peanut oil for flavour. Cook into a soup and serve.

CAUTION: *If suffering a deficiency of yin and a flushed feeling avoid eating this herb.*

CORIANDER
Coriandrum sativum L.
YAN SUI

The coriander, yan sui, is also called hu sui (foreign coriander), xiang sui (fragrant coriander) and yuan sui (garden coriander). It is an annual, but sometimes lives for two years and has a pungent aroma.

The root is spindle shaped, the stem cylindrical with many branches. The leaves are divided into a number of lobes and have a feathery appearance, the lobes being egg shaped or fan shaped, partly split. The edge of the leaf has blunt teeth, without any deep splits.

The leaves on the stem generally have three lobes with a feathery appearance. The flowers are white or pale violet. The fruit is round.

The fruit, branches and leaves are all used in medicine. Coriander contains protein, fat, carbohydrate, calcium, phosphorous, iron, carotene, vitamins B1, B2, C, niacin, aromatic camphor alcohol etc.

芫荽

The flavour of coriander is pungent, its nature warm and it affects the lungs and spleen.

PROPERTIES: Coriander can disperse cold feeling and promote sweating and clean a rash. The fruit helps regulate the flow of vital energy and strengthens the stomach.

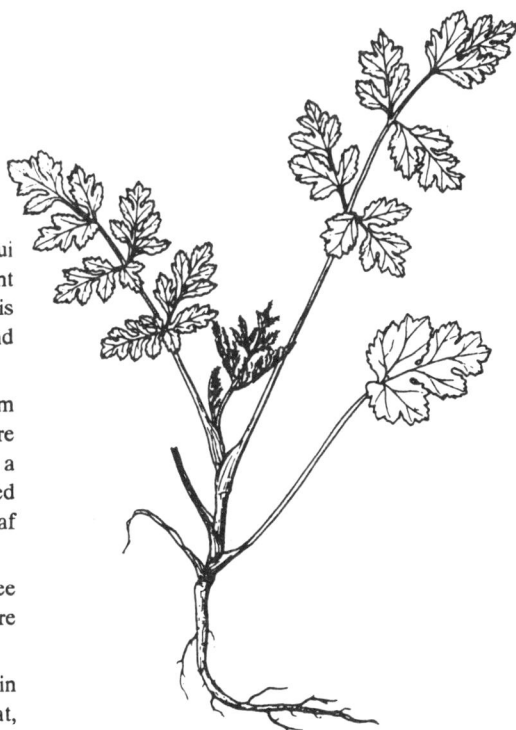

APPLICATIONS

1. INADEQUATE MEASLES ERUPTION. Take 10-15 grams of coriander, simmer in water and serve. At the same time take 30-60 grams of coriander, crush it and simmer in a little wine, then wrap in a cloth while still warm. Place the patient in a draught free area and use the cloth to rub the chest and back.

2. TIGHT, STUFFY FEELING IN THE CHEST. Take a quantity of coriander seed and crush it to a powder. At regular intervals take 10 grams in boiled water.

3. INDIGESTION, LOSS OF APPETITE. Take 6 grams of coriander seeds, 6 grams of dried orange peel, 10 grams of shen qu (a mixture of fermented powders consisting of red-knees herb, sweet wormwood, apricot kernel and wheat. It is used to promote digestion, regulate the middle-jiao, strengthen the spleen and regulate the function of the stomach) and 3 slices of fresh ginger. Simmer in water and serve.

4. TIGHT, OPPRESIVE FEELING IN THE CHEST; HERNIA PAIN. Take a quantity of coriander seeds and crush to a powder. At regular intervals take 10 grams of the powder and 10 grams of sugar, mix with warm boiled water and drink.

5. PROLAPSE OF THE ANUS. Take 500 grams of coriander and simmer it. Take advantage of the heat to squat over the container and let the steam treat the affected part.

6. FAVUS OF THE SCALP; TINEA CAPITUS IN CHILDREN. Take 10 grams of coriander seeds and 20 mls of camellia oil (oil expressed from the seed of *Camellia oleifera*)). Boil together for about 10 minutes and apply to the affected parts.

7. STOMACH ACHE WITH COLD FEELING IN STOMACH. Take 45 grams of coriander seeds, 45 grams of fennel seeds, 12 grams of calamus (*Acorus calamus*, sweet sedge), 12 grams of the root of Dutchman's pipe and 90 grams of cassia bark (Chinese cinnamon). Soak the ingredients in a litre of rice wine for 3 days and take 10 mls 3-4 times a day.

8. DIFFICULTY IN SWALLOWING; REGURGITATION, GASTRIC DISORDERS WITH NAUSEA. Take a "black meat" hen, pluck and dress it then stuff it with 30 grams of coriander seeds. Add water and simmer into a soup. Several times a day eat some of the meat and drink some soup.

CAUTION: *Persons suffering from beriberi, incised wounds or deficient yin should avoid this plant.*

THORNY CORIANDER
Eryngium foetidum L.
CI YAN SUI

The thorny coriander, ci yan sui, is also called yang yan sui (foreign coriander), jia yan sui (false coriander) and shan yan sui (mountain coriander). The plant may be biennial or perennial and has a fragrant smell. The main root is spindle shaped and the stem is green and robust. The leaves are narrow, pointed and inverted eg shaped. The upper leaves grow opposite each other and do not have stalks.

刺芫荽

The flowers are white or pale yellow. The fruit is ett shaped or round, and the surface has tumour-like projections. The whole plant is used in medicine. It contains a small amount of volatile substance.

The flavour is pungent and slightly bitter, its nature warm and it affects the lungs. It can dissipate wind, help clear a rash, disperse poison and the aromatic properties invigorate the stomach.

APPLICATIONS

1. COMMON COLD WITH CHEST PAINS; COUGH; MEASLES IN SMALL CHILDREN. Take 10-15 grams of thorny coriander, simmer in water and serve.

2. INDIGESTION, LOSS OF APPETITE. Take 15 grams of thorny coriander, simmer in water and serve. Another treatment is to take an appropriate amount of thorny coriander, chop it and dress with sesame oil and salt, then eat as a gold dish.

3. PAINFUL SWELLINGS FROM FALLS AND SIMILAR ACCIDENTS. Take an appropriate amount of thorny coriander, wash clean, crush it and obtain the juice. Add a small measure of rice wine and drink. Apply the sediment to the affected parts as a dressing.

CAUTION: *Persons suffering from a deficiency of yin with a feverish feeling should avoid this plant.*

GINGER
Zingiber officinale Rosc.
JIANG

Ginger, jiang, is also called sheng jiang (raw ginger), gan jiang (dry ginger) and bao jiang. It is a perennial root vegetable. The rhizome is thick and irregular in shape, cream coloured and with a distinctive ginger smell.

The leaves are narrow and pointed, 15-30mm wide. The flowers grow on the spike. The rhizome is used in medicine. It contains volatile oils, ginger alcohol, zingiberene fenchylene, borneol, cajeputol, etc. It also contains a small amount of ginerol as well as protein, fat, calcium, phosphorous, iron, vitamin C and a small measure of vitamins B1 and B2.

The flavour of the ginger is pungent, its nature warm and it affects the lungs, spleen and stomach. It can induce sweating, disperse cold, warm the stomach and neutralize poison.

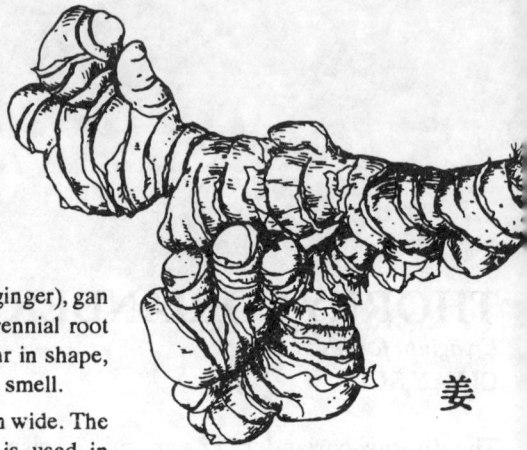

APPLICATIONS

1. COUGH ASSOCIATED WITH A COLD, EXCESSIVE FROTHY PHLEGM. Take 10 grams of fresh ginger, 6 spring onions, and a Chinese radish. Clean the radish and then boil it. Add the ginger and spring onions and boil to make one bowlful. Take this in one serve. Also take some ginger, simmer it and while still warm rub it on the patients back.

2. COUGHING WITH EXCESSIVE FROTHY PHLEGM. Take half a small cup of fresh ginger juice and 30 mls of honey. Blend together and serve. Another treatment is to take 10 grams of dried ginger, 30 grams of coriander and 3 grams of bitter apricot kernels. Simmer in water and serve.

3. COLD PAIN IN THE STOMACH WITH VOMITING AND DIARRHOEA. Take 30 grams of fresh ginger and 120 grams of garlic. Wash clean and crush to obtain the juice. Take in one serve.

4. STOMACH ACHE WITH A COLD FEELING IN THE STOMACH, PALE LIPS, VOMITING WITH EXCESSIVE SALIVA. Take 6 grams of fresh ginger and 10 grams of black pepper. Grind to a powder and divide into two serves. Take in warm boiled water.

5. STOMACH ACHE WITH COLD FEELING IN THE STOMACH, SOUR REGURGITATION, ACID VOMIT. Take 50 grams of fresh ginger and 15 grams of crushed cuttlefish bone. Add 200 mls of water and simmer. Divide into two doses and serve.

6. ROUNDWORM CAUSING OBSTRUCTION OF THE INTESTINES. Take 60 grams of fresh ginger, wash clean and crush to obtain the juice and add 60mls of honey. Divide into two or three serves. Reduce the amount for children.

7. HICCUPS. Take 6 grams of fresh ginger and 10 pieces of the calyx of persimmon. Simmer in water and serve.

8. PAIN IN THE LOWER PART OF THE STOMACH OR IN THE ABDOMEN DURING MENSTRUATION. Take 15 grams of fresh ginger and 2 green shelled duck eggs. Break the eggs into a pan, add the ginger and half a cup of wine and simmer. When cooked add a little raw sugar and serve.

9. POISONING FROM EATING PINELLIA TERNATA OR ARUM TRYPHYLLUM (JACK-IN-THE-PULPIT). Take 30 grams of fresh ginger, simmer in water and serve cold.

10. MIGRAINE. Take 6 grams of the skin of the ginger, 6 spring onions and half a cup of rice that has been used to make rice wine*. Crush together and then wrap the ingredients in gauze. Heat this and apply to the forehead and temples twice a day.

In the Chinese countryside the making of rice wine was once a common practise. The method is simple. Glutinous rice, or ordinary rice and sugar, is cooked then water and yeast added. The container is kept in a warm place and covered against the vinegar fly until fermenting has ceased. The rice can then be used as described above (Ed.).

11. SKIN PEELING OFF HANDS. Take 30 grams of fresh ginger, slice fine and soak in 75mls of wine for 24 hours. Apply this to the skin twice a day.

12. BALDNESS. Take a piece of fresh ginger and simmer till cooked. Slice it open while it is still warm and rub it on the bald spot.

13. RED OR WHITE VITILIGO; RED OR WHITE PATCHES ON THE SKIN. Crush some ginger and obtain the juice. Rub this frequently on the affected parts.

14. INJURIES FROM FALLS AND SPRAINS. Crush some ginger to obtain the juice, add some wine and rub on the affected parts.

CAUTION; *If suffering from a hot feeling due to a deficiency of yin, avoid eating ginger.*

SAND GINGER

GALANGA
Kaempferia galanga L.
SHA JIANG

The sand ginger, sha jiang, is also called shan nai (mountain how) and san nai (three how). It is a perennial small herb iwthout a stem. The rhizome is thick and may grow singly or in clumps, it is pale green or greenish white and has a fragrant flavour. The leaf is often divided into two parts and is almost round. The flower is white.

The rhizome is used in medicine. It contains volatile oils, protein, starch and glutinous matter, etc.

沙姜

Its flavour is pungent, its nature warm and it affects the stomach. It can warm the interior, dispel humid moisture, promote vital energy and help relieve pain.

APPLICATIONS

1. PAIN DUE TO INJURIES FROM FALLS, SPRAINS AND WOUNDS. Take 10 grams of sand ginger and crush fine. Divide into three parts and take with white wine in the course of a day.

2. SPLINTERS OF METAL, BAMBOO, WOOD OR GLASS IN THE FLESH. Take 10 grams of sand ginger, 10 grams of root of *Achyranthes bidentata* and 30 grams of sour Chinese onion heads. Crush together, apply to the affected place and cover with a bandage.

CAUTION: *If suffering from anemia due to a deficiency of yin or "stagnant fire" in the stomach avoid this vegetable.*

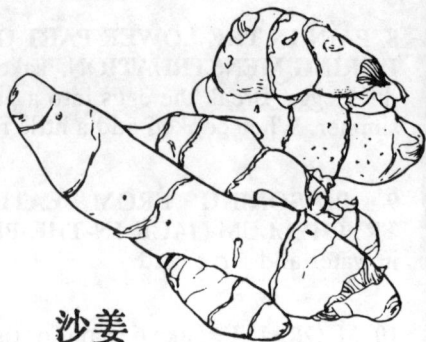

SPRING ONIONS

SCALLIONS, WELSH ONION
Allium fistulosum L.
CONG

Spring onions, cong, are also called da cong (great onion) and hu cong (foreign onion). The plant lives for many years and has a characteristic onion smell. The bulb grows singly and is cylindrical. The outer skin is generally white but sometimes pale red-brown and thin.

The leaves are cylindrical and hollow and generally 5mm or more in diameter. The umbel is ball shaped with many white flowers.

The whole plant is used in medicine. It contains

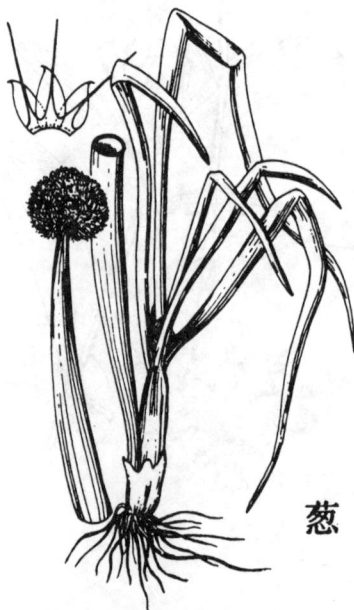

葱

volatile oils, vitamins C, B1, B2, niacin, as well as a small amount of vitamin A, fat, glutinous matter, etc.

The flavour is pungent, its nature warm, and it affects lungs and stomach. It can induce sweating, invigorate the yang and profit urine.

APPLICATIONS

1. COMMON COLD WITH HEADACHE AND DRY HEAT. Take 10 complete spring onions, 15 grams of fermented soya beans (dou chi) plus 2 bowls of water. Simmer together till reduced to one bowl and serve it while it is still warm. After eating the patient should be covered with a quilt or blanket in order to sweat a little.

Another treatment is to take 20 complete spring onions and an appropriate quantity of rice and simmer into a porridge. Add a small amount of vinegar and serve it while it is still warm. After eating wrap the patient in blankets in order to induce sweating.

2. BREASTS SWOLLEN AND PAINFUL, DIFFICULTY IN EXPRESSING MILK. Take an appropriate amount of the lower part of spring onions, crush, add a little salt and stir fry. While still warm press and bind the pulp onto the breasts.

3. DIFFICULTY IN PASSING URINE, ISCHURIA. Take 100 grams of spring onions, wash clean and crush. Add a little salt and stir fry. While still hot press to the navel. Re-heat and repeat several times.

4. "WIND MOIST" PAIN, PAIN THOUGHT TO BE CAUSED BY WIND AND MOISTURE, SWELLINGS CAUSED BY FALLS AND SIMILAR ACCIDENTS. Take a bunch of sping onions and crush. Add a little wine, stir-fry it till hot and press to the affected parts.

5. FROST-BITE. Take 100 grams of roots of spring onions and 100 grams of the roots of eggplant. Simmer together and use the liquid to soak the affected parts.

6. PAINFUL SWOLLEN BOILS AND CARBUNCLES. Take an appropriate quantity of spring onions and crush them. Add a small amount of vinegar and stir-fry. When warm apply to the affected place and cover with a bandage.

CAUTION. *If constantly sweating or suffering from a flushed feeling due to a deficiency of yin, avoid this vegetable.*

GARLIC

Allium sativum L.

SUAN

Garlic, suan, is also called hu (calabash) and hu suan (calabash garlic). It is a perennial plant with a distinctive garlic flavour. The bulb is round or like a slightly flattened ball, and fleshy. The outer skin is a thin membrane of a number of layers, its colour white or violet.

The leaves are flat long narrow strips tapering to a point. The flowers are pink. The

bulb is used in medicine.

It contains protein, fat carbohydrate, calcuim, phosphorous, iron, vitamins B2, C, niacin, volatile oils and allicin.

Its flavour is pungent, its nature warm and it affects the spleen, stomach and lungs. It can warm the spleen, invigorate the stomach, promote vital energy, improve digestion, neutralize poison and eliminate worms.

蒜

EDITOR'S NOTE: The illustration shows a form of garlic not commonly seen in the west. Referring to this Herklots in Vegetables in South-East Asia *says "If very small garlic cloves are planted, or if growing conditions are poor, a single, small, solid clove, usually called a "round" is produced. . . . In the village markets of Hong Kong small rounds about the width of a thumbnail with a thin white, pink or light brown skin may be seen." So, although the illustration shows a form of garlic uncommon in the west, the text refers to common garlic as used in the west.*

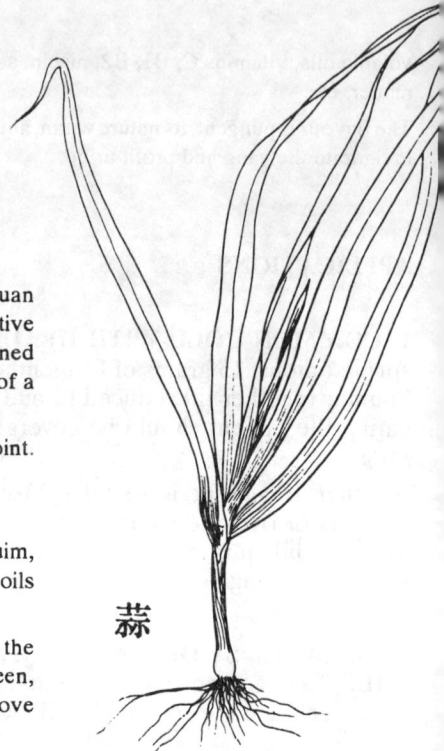

APPLICATIONS

1. PREVENTIVE MEASURES AGAINST THE COMMON COLD. Crush some garlic and obtain the juice. Add 10 parts of cool boiled water. Take drops of the solution in the nose at regular intervals.

2. PREVENTING EPIDEMIC CEREBROSPINAL MENINGITIS. Take 5 grams of garlic (proportionally less for children) and eat at meals. After the meal rinse the mouth with salted water. Do this for 3 days. Another treatments is to take 15 grams of garlic, remove the skins, crush and add 40mls of water plus an appropriate measure of sugar. Divide into 2 doses and serve during the day. REpeat this for 5 days.

3. TUBERCULOSIS. Take 30 grams of purple skinned garlic and discard the skins, add 3 grams of baiji powder made from the tuber of the hyacinth bletilla *(Rhizoma Bletillae)*. First take the garlic and place in boiling water for one minute and then scoop out (it need only be partly cooked). Take 30 grams of rice, place in the garlic water and cook into rice gruel. Add the garlic and baiji powder to the rice gruel and eat after a meal. Do this daily. In

addition 4-5 cloves of garlic may be eaten daily for 100 days.

4. WHOOPING COUGH. Take 30 grams of purple skinned garlic, discard the skin and crush. Add a small cup of warm boiled water and allow to soak for 5-6 hours then add an appropriate quantity of sugar. For children under 3 serve 1/2 a spoonful, and for 3-5 a full spoon. Do this 3 times a day.

5. PREVENTION OF DYSENTERY. Take 10 grams of garlic, discard the skins and crush. then soak in 100mls of warm boiled water for 6 hours. Add an appropriate measure of sugar, divide into three doses and take these in the course of a day.

6. DYSENTERY. Take five grams of garlic and discard the skins. Eat this in small amounts over the course of a day, and repeat this daily for 5-6 days.

7. ACUTE GASTROENTERITIS. Take 6 grams of garlic and discard the skins, add an appropriate amount of salt and crush together. Pour warm boiled water over the garlic and serve one or two tijmes a day. Repeat this for several days. Alternatively take an appropriate quantity of garlic and crush it then bind this to the navel and to the sole of the foot.

8. ASCITES DUE TO CIRRHOSIS OF THE LIVER. Cook an appropriate quantity of garlic in peanut oil and eat as a vegetable at meals. Do this for 2-3 months.

9. NOSEBLEEDING, EPISTAXIS. Take 10 grams of garlic, crush and bind to the centre of the sole of the foot. If bleeding from the fight nostril bind to the right foot, if from the left nostril then bind to the left foot. If both nostrils - then both feet. The bleeding does not stop until the soles of the feet feel quite hot.

10. CENTIPEDE BITE. Crush some garlic and apply to the bite.

11. BOILS; FURUNCLE; INNOMINATE TOXIC SWELLING. Take some garlic, crush, apply to the affected place and cover with a bandage.

12. CORNS. Take equal quantities of garlic and spring onion and crush together into a paste. Just before it is to be used, add a little vinegar. Disinfect the area around the corn and then trim it down with a sharp knife as far as possible, but stop before it bleeds.
Soak the area in lightly salted water for 20 minutes until the corn becomes soft then apply the garlic and onion mixture and cover it with a bandage. Change the dressing and repeat the treatment daily or every second day. The corn will usually be healed in 5-7 days.

13. PREVENTING AND TREATING LEAD POISONING. Take 6 grams of raw garlic and eat twice a day.

CAUTION: *If suffering from a deficiency of yin with hot flushes, avoid this vegetable.*

HOT PEPPERS
CHILLI, CAYENNE PEPPER,
PAPRIKA

Capsicum annuum L.
LA JIAO

The hot pepper or chilli, la jiao, is also called la zi (hot
pepper chilli) and fan jiao (foreign pepper). It is
generally an annual but sometimes lives for a number
of years.

The leaves may be oval, egg shaped or pointed. The
flowers grow singly, they are white and hang
downwards. The fruit is long, finger shaped and green
when immature. On ripening it may be red, orange or
purple-red.

Because this plant has been cultivated over a long
period many varieties have developed which differ
from each other in shape and appearance.

The fruit, roots and stem are all used in medicine. The
fruit contains protein, fat, carbohydrate, calcium,
phosphorous, iron, carotene, vitamins B1, B2, C, niacin, chilli alkali, citric acid, tartaric acid, malic
acid, etc.

辣椒

The flavour of the fruit is pungent, its nature hot and it affects the heart and spleen. It can warm
the internal organs, invigorate the stomach, aid digestion, act as a blood tonic and diminish
swelling.

APPLICATIONS

**1. STOMACH ACHE WITH A COLD FEELING IN THE STOMACH; SWOLLEN
STOMACH CAUSED BY LOSS OF VITAL ENERGY.** Mix an appropriate quantity
of hot peppers in with the vegetable dishes and eat daily.

2. UNDER-ARM ODOUR. Obtain the most pungent hot peppers or chillis available,
chop fine and put into a bottle. Add 20mls of 2-2.5% tincture of iodine. Shake well
before applying. Use cotton wool to wipe under the arms daily 1-3 times.

3.FROST-BITE THAT HAS NOT BEGUN TO FESTER; CHILBLAINS. Put some
crushed peppers i;nto sesame oil and cook to make pepper oil. Apply this oil to the
affected parts daily 1 or 2 times.

4. MENORRHAGIA. Take 60 grams of hot peppers and 2-4 hen's feet. Add water
and simmer until cooked. Divide into 2 doses and serve in the course of a day. Repeat
this for 5-10 days.

**5. PROLONGED ANEMIA CAUSED BY MALARIA; CONSTANT COLD
FEELING.** Take 60 grams of hot peppers and 60 grams of dog meat. Add water and
simmer until cooked, then puree the meat and peppers. Drink the soup and eat the
meat.

CAUTION: *People suffering from tuberculosis, duodenal ulcers, bronchitis, hepatitis,
gall bladder and kidney ailments, should avoid this vegetable.*

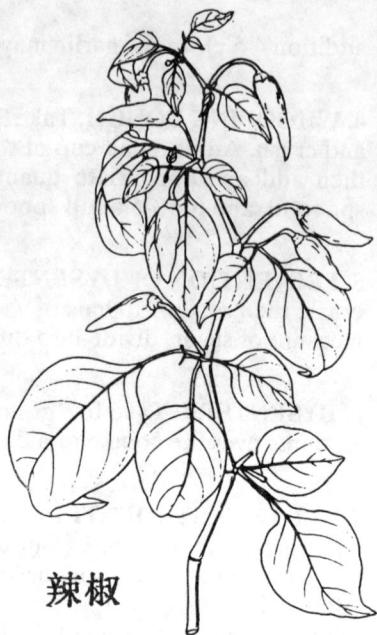

PEPPER
Piper nigrum
HU JIAO

Pepper, hu jiao (foreign pepper) is also called bai hu jiao (white foreign pepper), hei hu jiao (black foreign pepper), bai chuan (white river/sichuan) and gu yue (ancient moon).

It is a climbing woody vine, with swollen joints on the stem. The leaf has a leathery quality and varies from egg shaped to elongated egg shape. The inflorescence grows opposite the leaves and the flowers are polygamous.

The berry is round, without a stem, its diameter 3-4 millimetres. Immature berries turn black when dried, while ripe berries turn red.

胡椒

The berry is used in medicine. It contains pepper alkali, volatile oils, etc. Its flavour is pungent, its nature hot, and it affects the stomach and large intestine. Pepper can warm the internal organs, disperse cold, regulate vital energy and ease pain.

APPLICATIONS

1. STOMACH ACHE WITH A COLD FEELING IN THE STOMACH, COLOURLESS LIPS, VOMITING CLEAR LIQUID. Take 3-5 grams of peppercorns, crush to powder, add to wine and serve.

2. VOMITING AFTER EATING. Take a gram of ground pepper, add to ginger soup and serve.

3. PAIN DUE TO GALL STONES. Take equal quantities of pepper and soduim sulfate crystals and grind together into a powder. Each day take 3 grams in warm boiled water.

4. COMBINED INDIGESTION AND DIARRHOEA IN SMALL CHILDREN. Take 1 gram of white ground pepper and 9 grams of glucose powder and mix together. For children under a year of age serve only 0.3-0.5 grams, up to the age of 3, 0.5-1.5 grams and for older children no more than 2 grams. Mix together with boiled water and serve 3 times a day for 1-3 days.

5. CHRONIC NEPHRITIS. Take 7 peppercorns of white pepper and a hen's egg. Make a small hole in the egg and put the peppercorns inside. Wrap the egg in damp paper to steam it until cooked, then discard the shell and eat the egg and peppers. Adults should do this twice a day, children once a day. Repeat this for 10 days as a course of treatment. After 3 days again repeat the treatment for 10 days. This is usually done 3 times.

6. STOMACH ACHE WITH A COLD FEELING IN THE STOMACH. Take 10 peppercorns of white pepper and grind to a powder. Add this to wine and serve.

7. DEFICIENCY OF VITAL ENERGY IN THE AGED; PROLAPSE OF THE ANUS. Take 70 peppercorns and a length of clean, washed pig's intestine. Put the peppers into the intestine, tie up both ends, place in water and cook. When cooked pulp the sausage and serve.

8. LEUCORRHOEA, WHITES WITH A WATERY DISCHARGE; FEAR OF COLD: PALE COLOURLESS FACE. Take 7 peppercorns and a hen's egg. Make a small hole in the egg, put the peppercorns into the egg, wrap in moist paper and

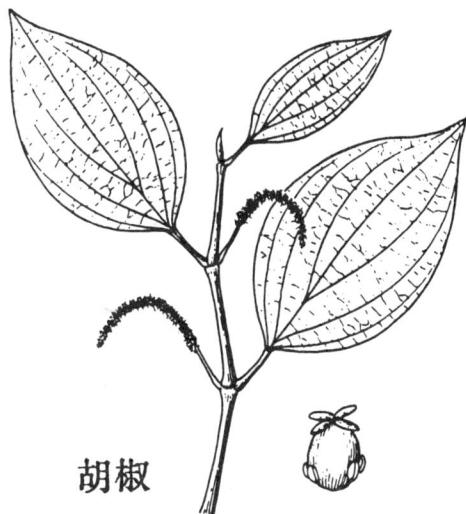

simmer in water until it is cooked. Discard the shell and eat the egg and pepper. Do this daily and continue for 5-7 days.

9. MALARIA ACCOMPANIED BY A CONSTANT COLD FEELING. Take 20 white peppercorns and roughly crush them. Steam until cooked then add to wine.

10. EXZEMA OF THE SCROTUM. Take 5 grams of pepper and soak in 50mls of white wine (vodka may be used. Ed.) for a week. After a week has passed strain the liquid and it is ready for use. Rub the liquid on the affected parts daily, 2 or 3 times.

CAUTION: *If suffering from a dry flushed feeling due to a deficiency of yin avoid this condiment.*

FALSE PEPPER
Piper sarmentosum Roxb.
JIA JU

False pepper, jia ju, is also called ge ju (clam pepper) and jia lou. It is a perennial creeper with roots growing on each node. The leaves are thin and the veins that grow on the back of the leaves are covered with short powdery hairs.

The flowers grow in a grain-like spike opposite the leaves. The male flowers are 15-20mm long, the female flowers 6-8mm long.

The berry is almost round and without hairs. The whole plant is used in medicine. Its flavour is pungent, its nature warm, and it affects the lungs and spleen. It can warm the internal organs, disperse cold, dispel wind, help retain body moisture, diminish swelling and ease pain.

假蒟

APPLICATIONS

1. STOMACH ACHE WITH COLD FEELING IN THE STOMACH; SWOLLEN ABDOMEN; LOSS OF APPETITE. Take 30 grams of false pepper and some lean pork or a hen's egg. Add vegetables, cook into a soup and serve.

2. COUGH DUE TO WIND AND COLD. Take 30 grams of the leaves of the false pepper and 100 grams of pig's blood. Eat with vegetables as part of a meal.

3. DROPSY, OEDEMA, ALL OVER THE BODY. Take 20 grams of the leaves of the false pepper, 20 grams each of cowpeas, mung beans and small red beans, plus a garlic bulb and 15 grams of glutinous rice. Add water and simmer until cooked, then add a little sugar for flavour. Eat one bowlful twice a day for 3-5 days.

4. SWOLLEN FEET IN WOMEN AFTER GIVING BIRTH. Take 30 grams of false peppers and a codfish head. Cook together in water and add a little sesame oil and salt for flavour. In addition take a quantity of the whole plant, simmer in water and use the liquid to wash the feet.

5. THRUSH OF THE MOUTH IN SMALL CHILDREN. Take a few leaves of the false pepper, simmer in water and use the liquid to wash the mouth area.

6. NIGHT BLINDNESS. Take 15 grams of false pepper and 60 grams of pork liver. Simmer together and eat. Do this once or twice a day for 3 days.

7. PAINFUL JOINTS DUE TO RHEUMATISM. Take 30 grams of the leaves of false

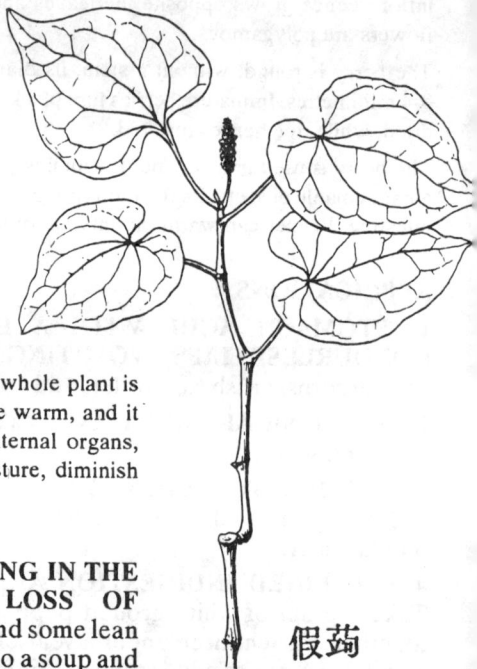

pepper. Simmer in water, add a little wine and serve. In addition take some leaves and stems of the plant, simmer in water and use the liquid to wash the affected parts.

8. ECZEMA OF THE SCROTUM. Take a quantity of leaves and a stem of the false pepper, simmer in water and wash the affected parts.

CAUTION: *Persons suffering from a hot dry feeling due to a deficiency of vital energy should avoid eating this plant.*

PEPPERMINT
Mentha haplocalyx
BO HE

Peppermint, bo he, is also called wild mint, family mint and local mint. It is a perennial herb. The stem is vertical with many branches; the upper part covered with fine soft hairs, the lower part with fine hair only on the angularities.

The leaves grow opposite and are usually oval and pointed, more rarely oval. The edge of the leaf is roughly saw toothed.

The flowers are pale violet. The whole plant is used in medicine.

It contains peppermint oil, peppermint camphor and menthone. Its flavour is pungent, its nature cool and it affects the liver and lungs. It helps expel wind and acts as a tonic to refresh the system.

薄荷

APPLICATIONS

1. COMMON COLD WITH STUFFY NOSE; HEADACHE; SLIGHT AVERSION TO COLD; INABILITY TO SWEAT; ANHIDROSIS. Take 10 grams of peppermint, 5 spring onions, 3 slices of fresh ginger and 10 grams of light fermented soya beans. Simmer in water and serve.

2. FEVER WITH HEADACHE; ACHING JOINTS IN THE WHOLE BODY; AVERSION TO COLD IN THE BACK; ANHIDROSIS; INABILITY TO SWEAT. Take 12 grams of peppermint leaves, 10 grams of the discarded shells of cicadas, 20 grams of gypsum and 6 grams of licorice. Simmer in water and serve.

3. SORE THROAT; EXCESSIVE PHLEGM. Take 15 grams of peppermint, simmer in water, add a little sugar and serve.

4. HOARSENESS DUE TO SHOUTING, TALKING OR SINGING. Take 10 grams of peppermint and 3 grams of natural indigo powder *(Indigo Naturalis)*. Simmer the peppermint in water, add the powder and serve twice a day.

5. SKIN PRURITUS. Take 10 grams of peppermint, add 10 grams of the discarded shells of the cicada. Simmer in water and serve.

6. BEE STING. Crush some peppermint, obtain the juice and rub on the affected part.

CAUTION: *Persons suffering from a deficiency of vital energy should avoid this herb.*

SPEARMINT

Mentha spicata

LIU LAN XIANG

Spearmint, liu lan xiang (remain orchid fragrant) is also called lu bo he (green peppermint), jia bo he (false peppermint) gou rou xiang (dog flesh fragrance) and yu xiang cai (fish fragrance vegetable). It is a perennial herb.

The leaves grow opposite each other with little or no stalks. They are egg shaped or pointed, without hairs or with very few hairs.

The flowers grow in clusters on a spike 40-100mm long and are pale violet in colour.

The whole plant is used in medicine. It contains volatile oils, limonene and phellandrene.

Its flavour is pungent, its nature cool and it affects the liver, lungs and stomach. It can cool a fever, dispel wind, stop coughing, decrease swelling and neutralize poison.

留兰香

APPLICATIONS

1. COMMON COLD. Take 15 grams of spearmint and 3 slices of fresh ginger. Simmer together in water and serve.

2. COUGH CAUSED BY THE WIND, WITH EXCESSIVE PHLEGM. Take 30 grams of spearmint and simmer in water. Add a little sugar and drink as a tea.

3. STOMACH ACHE. Take 15 grams of spearmint, 10 grams of fennel seeds, 6 grams of dried orange peel and 3 slices of ginger. Simmer in water and serve.

4. NERVOUS HEADACHE, TENSION HEADACHE. Take 15 grams of spearmint and 15 grams of red Chinese dates. Simmer in water and serve.

5. SORE EYES DUE TO GLARE; CONJUNCTIVITIS. Take some spearmint and crush to obtain the juice. Strain this and put a few drops in the eye.

6. NOSE BLEEDING. Take 30 grams of cogongrass roots *(Imperata cylindrica)* (quangxi and 15 grams of spearmint, simmer in water.

7.CHAPPED SKIN. Take some spearmint, crush it and obtain the juice, then rub this on the affected parts.

8. BOILS. Crush some spearmint and place on the boil, covering it with a plaster or bandage.

CAUTION: *Persons suffering from a lack of vital energy should avoid this herb.*

PURPLE PERILLA

Perilla frutescens var. crispa

ZI SU

The purple perilla, zi su, is also called bai su (white perilla), hong su (red perilla) and ji guan zi su (cockscomb purple perilla). It is an annual plant. The stem is vertical and green or purple, covered with thick long flexible hairs.

The leaves grow opposite each other and are egg shaped or round, the edges roughly serrated. Both sides may be either green or purple, but in some varieties only the underside of the leaf is purple. The flowers grow in clusters on spikes and are white or reddish-purple.

The leaf, stem and fruit are all used in medicine.

The leaf contains volatile oils, fat, vitamin B1, perilla aldehyde, arginine, eugenol oil. Its flavour is pungent, its nature warm and it affects the lungs and spleen. It can dispel cold feelings, promote the circulation of vital energy, warm the internal organs and help relieve the effects of fish and crab poisoning.

紫苏

APPLICATIONS

1. COMMON COLD. Take 10 grams of perilla leaves, 10 spring onions and 3 slices of fresh ginger. Simmer in water and serve.

2. CHILL AND HEADACHE CAUSED BY EXTERNAL FACTORS. Take 10 grams of perilla, 6 grams of cassia bark (osmanthus fragrans Lour.) and 5 spring onions. Simmer in water and serve.

3. ACUTE GASTROENTERITIS. Take 10 grams of perilla leaves, 10 grams of wrikled giant hysop (Agastache rugosa), 6 grams of dried orange peel and 3 slices of fresh ginger. Simmer in water and serve.

4. TIGHT, SUFFOCATING FEELING IN THE CHEST; HICCUPS. Take 15 grams of perilla stalks, 6 grams of dried orange peel and 3 slices of fresh ginger. Simmer in water and serve.

5. RESTLESS MOVEMENTS OF UNBORN CHILD. Take 30 grams of ramie roots and 10 grams of perilla stalks. Simmer in water and serve.

6. NAUSEA AND VOMITING DURING PREGNANCY. Take 15 grams of perilla leaves and 3 grams of the rhizome of Chinese goldthread (Coptis chinensis). Simmer in water and serve.

7. OEDEMA; DROPSY. Take 20 grams of perilla stalks, a bulb of garlic with the skin attached, 15 grams of the skin of mature ginger and 15 grams of the skin of winter melons. Simmer in water and serve.

8. FOOD POISONING FROM EATING CRAB. Take 30 grams of perilla leaves and 3 slices of fresh ginger. Simmer with water into a soup and drink frequently.

9. ECZEMA OF THE SCROTUM. Take some perilla leaves, simmer in water and wash the affected parts.

CAUTION: *Persons suffering from a common cold should avoid this plant.*

SWEET BASIL

Ocimum Basilicum
LUO LE

Sweet basil, luo le (net/spread out rein in/carve) is also called ling ling xiang (zero mound fragrant), xiang cao (fragrant grass) and jiu ceng to (nine storied tower). It is an annual herbaceous plant. The leaves grow opposite each other and are egg shaped or an elongated egg shape 25-50mm long and 10-25mm wide, both surfaces are green.

The flowers are only 6mm long and pale violet. The seeds are smooth and brown-black in colour.

The whole plant is used in medicine. The stem, leaves and flower clusters contain estragole, linalyl acetate, clove phenol, etc. The fruit contains protein, fat and carbohydrates.

Its flavour is pungent, its nature warm, and it affects the lungs, spleen, stomach and large intestine.

It can induce sweating, dispel wind, help moisten internal organs, cleanse the blood and ease pain.

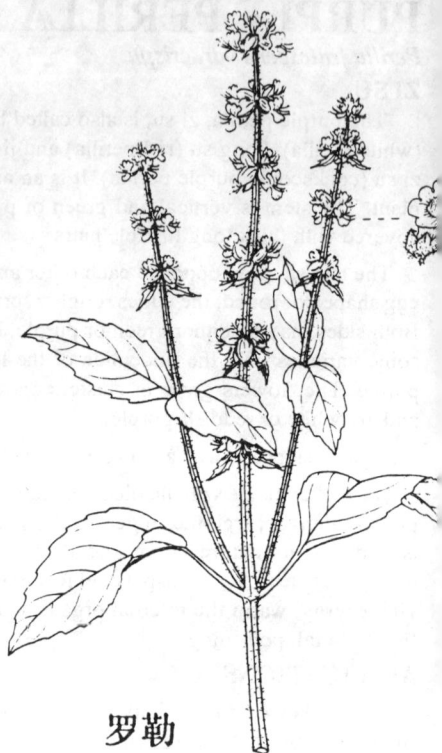

APPLICATIONS

罗勒

1. COMMON COLD; HEADACHE; TIGHT FEELING IN THE CHEST. Take 30 grams of sweet basil and 6 grams of fresh ginger. Simmer in water and serve.

2. FLATULENCE IN HOT WEATHER; TIGHT FEELING IN THE CHEST; BAD BREATH. Take 15 grams of sweet basil, 10 grams of perilla stalks, 10 grams of the tuber of the dwarf lilyturf *(Ophiopogon japonicus)* and 10 grams of rice sprouts. Simmer in water and serve.

3. AMENORRHOEA OR IMPEDED MENSTRUAL FLOW. Take 30 grams of sweet basil and 15 grams of red-rooted salvia *(salvia miltiorrhiza)*. Simmer in water and serve.

4. THEUMATIC JOINT PAIN; SWELLING DUE TO FALLS AND SIMILAR INJURIES. Take some sweet basil, simmer in water and wash the affected parts.

5. ECZEMA. Take some sweet basil, simmer in water and wash the affected parts.

CAUTION: *Persons suffering from a lack of vital energy and poor circulation should avoid this herb.*

PURSLANE

Portulaca oleracea L.
MA CHI XIAN

Purslane is a common weed in gardens all over the world and has been used as a vegetable for centuries. A note in the Journal of the New York Botanical Garden for 1942 reads "In my opinion the young leaves and stems when cooked about 15 minutes in boiling salted water are far better than spinach or Swiss chard". Ed.

Purslane, ma chi xian (horse tooth amaranth) is also called gua zi cai (melon seed vegetable), ma chi cai (horse tooth vegetable) and wu hang cai (five lines grass). It is a fleshly herbaceous annual plant, without hair. The stem is usually reddish purple in colour.

The leaves are inverted egg shaped 10-25mm long. The flowers grow in groups of 2-3 on the tip of the branch and are yellow.

马齿苋

The seed capsule is conical, with a split cover. The seed is black and kidney shaped, with a wart like projection on it. The whole plant is used in medicine.

It contains a large measure of noradrenaline, sylvite, malic acid, citric acid, glutamic acid, alanine, sucrose, glucose, fructose, protein, fat, calcium, phosphorous, iron, carotene, vitamins B1, B2, C, niacin etc.

The flavour is slightly tart, its nature cool and it affects the large intestine, liver and spleen.

It can cool a fever, aid in poisoning, cool the blood, help stop bleeding, eliminate excessive body moisture, diminish swelling, kill fungus and help relieve dysentery.

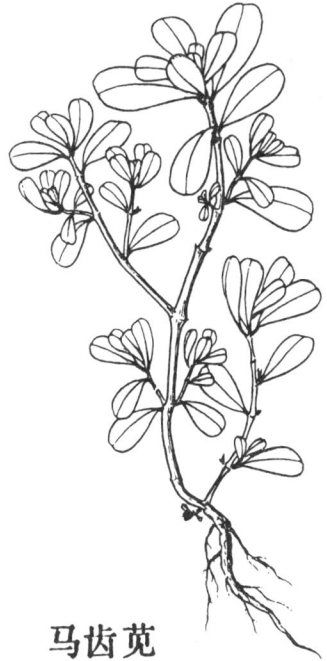

APPLICATIONS

1. PREVENTING BACTERIAL DYSENTERY. Take 500 grams of purslane, add one and a half litres of water and simmer till it has reduced to one half litre. The daily dose for an adult is 70 mls, proportionally reduced for children. Serve for 3-7 days.

2. BACTERIAL DYSENTERY. Take 750 grams of purslane, place in a covered pan without water and let it steam in its own juice for 3-4 minutes. Next crush it to obtain the juice, which should amount to about 150 mls. Take 50 mls 3 times a day. Another treatment is to take 120 grams of purslane and 60 grams of the tree cotton flowers *(Bombax malabaricum DC)*. Simmer in water and serve.

3. DYSENTERY AFTER MEASLES. Take 60 grams of purslane, add 200 mls of water and simmer till it has reduced to 100mls. Divide into 3 doses and serve in the course of a day.

4. ACUTE GASTROENTERITIS. Take 120 grams of purslane, simmer in water and add some honey. Divide in 3 doses and serve in the course of a day.

5. APPENDICITIS. Take 60 grams of purslane and 60 grams of dandelion. Simmer in water until it has reduced to a thick liquid of around 200 mls. Divide into 2 doses to take in the course of a day. Another treatment is to take 500 grams of purslane and wash it in warm boiled warm. Chew this raw, swallow the juice and then use the chewed remainder as a compress on the affected area.

6. HOOKWORM. Take 250 grams of purslane, add water and simmer to obtain a soup bowl of juice. Add 50mls of vinegar and some sugar and mix together. Take this on an empty stomach, and repeat for 3 days. Repeat the treatment after 10 days and again after another 10 days, 3 courses of treatment in all.

7. HAEMORRHOIDS. Take 250 grams of purslane and 250 grams of red-stemmed amaranthus *(Amaranthus spinosus L.)* simmer in water and serve. At the same time squat over a steaming bowl of the mixture, so that the steam can move over the affected parts.

8. PROLAPSE OF THE RECTUM IN SMALL CHILDREN CAUSED BY HOT MOIST CONDITIONS. Take 50 grams of purslane and a dried persimmon. Add 200 mls of water and simmer till it has reduced to 100 mls. Divide into 2 doses and serve in the course of a day.

9. WHOOPING COUGH IN SMALL CHILDREN. Take 50 grams of purslane, add 200 mls of water and simmer till reduced to 100 mls. Add some sugar and divide into 3 doses. Serve in the course of a day.

10. SIMPLE DIARRHOEA IN SMALL CHILDREN. Take 100 grams of purslane, add 300 mls of water and simmer till reduced to 100 mls. Add some sugar and serve in several small doses in the course of a day.

11. LUNG ULCERATION, PUS ON THE LUNGS. Take 500 grams of purslane, wash in boiled water and crush to obtain the juice the add some honey. Serve this daily and continue the treatment for 2 weeks.

12. PULMONARY TUBERCULOSIS. Take 250 grams of purslane, simmer in water until cooked, divide into 3 parts and serve in the course of a day. Continue this treatment for 1-4 months.

13. HEPATITIS. Take 250 grams of purslane and 30 grams of *Hydro cotyle sidthorpiodes Lam.* (a type of pennywort). Simmer in water and drink as a tea. Continue this treatment for 5-10 days.

14. ACUTE INFECTION OF URINARY TRACT. Take 250 grams of purslane, add 200 mls of water and simmer till reduced to 100 mls. Add some sugar and divide into 3 doses. Serve in the course of a day.

15. LARYNGITIS. Take 250 grams of purslane, wash clean and crush to obtain the juice. Use this frequently as a gragle.

16. BEGINNING OF HEMIPLEGIA. Take 250 grams of purslane and 200 grams of snakehead fish, add 300 mls of water and simmer till reduced to 100 mls. Eat this at one serve and repeat for 5-7 days.

17. DYSENTERY AFTER GIVING BIRTH; DIFFICULTY IN PASSING URINE; PAIN IN NAVEL AND ABDOMEN. Take 500 grams of purslane, wash clean and crush to obtain the juice, add some honey and drink.

18. PUERPERAL FEVER. Take 120 grams of purslane and 60 grams of dandelion, simmer in water and serve.

19. BLEEDING FROM THE VAGINA. Take 60 grams of purslane and 60 grams of clam meat, simmer in water and serve.

20. LEUCORRHOEA. Take 500 grams of purslane, wash and crush to obtain the juice. Break an egg into this and steam until the egg is cooked, then serve. Repeat for 3-5 days.

21. MASTITIS. Take some purslane, wash clean and crush it. Add csome brown sugar and apply to the breasts as a dressing. Change this dressing daily for 2-3 days.

22. (HERPES) ZOSTER. Take some purslane, wash clean and crush to obtain the juice. Apply this to the affected parts.

23. ANUS SWOLLEN AND PAINFUL. Take a quantity of purslane and creeping oxalis *(Oxalis corniculata)*. Simmer together in water, squat over the steam and also use the liquid to wash the area.

24. INFECTED SORES. Take some purslane, wash and add brown sugar or salt. Crush together and use this as a dressing on the affected parts.

CAUTION: *Persons suffering cold, empty feelings in the spleen and stomach should avoid purslane.*

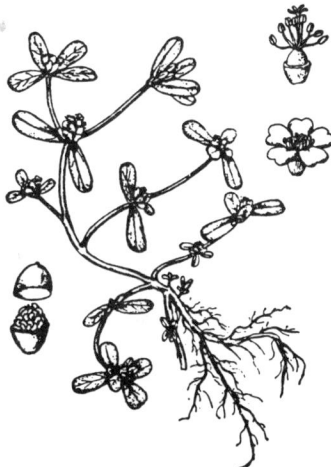

SHEPHERD'S PURSE

Capsella bursa-pastoris (L.) Medic.

JI CAI

Shepherd's purse, ji cai, is also called ji, di cai (earth vegetable), ji yi cai (hen's wing vegetable), jiao zi cai (dumpling vegetable), shang ji cai (upper self vegetable) and hu sheng cao (protect life grass). It is usually an annual, but sometimes lives for 2 years.

The stem is vertical and has branches. The leaves at the base of the plant grow closely together but are sparse on the upper parts. They are long and narrow with a serrated edge, and the base of the leaf wraps around the plant stalk.

The flower is white. The seed is long, oval and pale brown. The whole plant is used in medicine. It contains malic acid, oxalic acid, tartaric acid, fumaric acid, arginine, proline, methionine, leucine, glutamic acid, glycine, alanine, sucrox, glucose, lactose, potassium, calcium, sodium, iron, phosphorous etc.

荠菜

Its flavour is sweet, its nature cool and it affects the liver. It can cool fever, benefit the urine, cool the blood, help stop bleeding, calm the liver and nourish the yin.

APPLICATIONS

1. RENAL TUBERCULOSIS. Take 250 grams of shepherd's purse (or 30 grams of dried plant) add 3 bowls of water and simmer till it is reduced to 1 bowl. Break an egg into the liquid and boil until it is cooked and add a little salt for flavour. Eat the egg and drink the soup, in one or two serves, daily. Continue the treatment for 1 month.

2. TUBERCULOSIS AND COUGHING UP BLOOD. Take 60 grams of shepherd's purse and 15 grams of Chinese dates preserved in honey. Simmer in water and serve.

3. CHYLURIA. Take 250 grams of shepherd's purse and simmer in water. Divide into 3 parts and take daily. Repeat for 1-3 months.

4. HIGH BLOOD PRESSURE. Take 30 grams of shepherd's purse and 30 grams of selfheal (*Prunella vulgaris*). Simmer in water and serve.

5. DIZZINESS WITH SORE EYES. Take 60 grams of shepherd's purse and 10 grams of chrysanthemum flowers, simmer in water and serve.

6. DYSENTERY, DIARRHOEA. Take 100 grams of shepherd's purse, simmer in water, add brown sugar, and serve 3 times a day.

7. NEPHRITIS WITH DROPSY. Take 60 grams of shepherd's purse and 30 grams of Asiatic plantain (*Plantago asiatica*). Simmer in water and serve.

8. MEASLES IN CHILDREN. Take 30 grams of shepherd's purse and 30 grams of cogongrass root (*Imperata cylindrica*). Simmer in water and drink as a tea.

9. PREVENTING EPIDEMIC ENCEPHALITIS. Take 100 grams of shepherd's purse, simmer in water and drink as a tea.

10. UTERINE BLEEDING IN WOMEN; MENORRHAGIA. Take 30 grams of shepherd's purse and 30 grams of hairy-vein agrimony (*Agrimonia pilosa*), simmer in water and serve.

11. UTERINE BLEEDING; METRORRHAGIA. Take 30 grams of shepherd's purse and 30 grams of motherwort (*Leonurus heterophyllus*). Simmer in water and serve.

12. LEUCORRHOEA. Take 60 grams of shepherd's purse and some lean pork. Boil together with water into a soup, adding a little salt and sesame oil for flavour. Serve for a number of days.

13. WARDING OFF LICE AND FLEAS. Break up some shepherd's purse and place it under carpets and mats.

CAUTION: *Persons suffering from a cold feeling in the stomach should avoid this plant.*

INDIAN FIELDCRESS
Rorippa indica (L.) Hiern
HANG CAI

Indian fieldcress, hang cai, is also called ye you cai (wild oil vegetable), jiang jian dao cao (river scissors grass), tang ge cai (pond kudzu vine vegetable) and gan you cai (dry oil vegetable). It has a life of one or two years.

The stem is robust, without hairs or sometimes with a few hairs. The leaves are large and irregular. The flower is yellow. The seed pods are long cylinders holding two rows of seeds. The seeds are egg shaped and flat. The complete plant is used in medicine.

It contains rorifone and rorifone amide. The flavour is sweet and insipid, its nature cool and it affects the lungs and bladder. It can cool fever, disperse poison, stop coughing and promote diuresis.

蔊菜

APPLICATIONS

1. COUGH ASSOCIATED WITH A HOT FEELING IN THE LUNGS. Take 30 grams of the plant, simmer in water and serve.

2. DISEASES CAUSED BY WIND-HEAT. Take 30 grams of the plant and 5 spring onions. Simmer in water and serve warm.

3. FREQUENT URINATION WITH PAIN. Take 60 grams of the plant, and 30 grams of Asiatic plantain (*plantago major L.*). Simmer in water, add some brown sugar and serve.

4. DERMATITIS FROM PAINT. Crush the plant to obtain the juice and apply to the affected area.

CAUTION: *Persons suffering from a cold feeling in the stomach should avoid this plant.*

STINKING FISH PLANT
CORDATE HOUTTUYNIA
Houttuynia cordata Thunb.
YU XING CAO

The stinking fish plant, yu xing cao (fish smell grass), is also called ji cai, ce er gen (side ear root) and chou cao (stinking grass). It is a perennial that grows along the edge of streams and in damp areas. The lower part of the stem lies on the ground and roots grow from the nodes. The leaves are thick and roughly heart shaped with a wavy edge. The whole plant is used in medicine.

It contains volatile oil, potassium chloride, potassium sulfate, cordate houttuynia alkali quercitrin, etc. The flavour is slightly sour and pungent, its nature cold and it is good for the lungs. It can cool a fever, neutralize poison, promote diuresis and diminish swelling.

鱼腥草

APPLICATIONS

1. LOBAR PNEUMONIA. Take 60 grams of the plant and 30 grams of *Sarcandra glabra*. Simmer in water and serve.

2. LUNG ULCERATION. Take 60 grams of the plant, pour a bowl of water over this and let it soak for an hour. Bring to the boil then remove from the heat and serve warm.

3. HOT COUGH. Take 60 grams of the plant, simmer in water, add some sugar and serve.

4. COUGHING PUS AND BLOOD DUE TO PUMONARY ABSCESS. Take 60 grams of the plant and 250 grams of pork lung. Boil with water into a soup and add a little salt and sesame oil for flavour. Eat the meat and drink the soup.

5. DYSENTERY AND VOMITING CAUSED BY HOT WEATHER. Take 30 grams of the plant, simmer in water, add a little brown sugar and serve.

6. SUNSTROKE. Take 100 grams of the plant, wash clean and crush to obtain the juice. Mix with boiled water and serve.

7. ACUTE PROSTATITIS, INFLAMATION OF THE PROSTRATE GLAND. Take 60 grams of the plant root, crush it, then soak it for 1 hour in a bowl of the water that has been used to wash rice for the second time. Discard the sediment and serve the liquid twice a day for 3-5 days.

8. INFECTION OF THE URINARY PASSAGE. Take 100 grams of the plant, simmer in water, add some sugar and serve.

9. CHICKEN POX. Take 30 grams of the plant and 10 grams of Chinese violet (*Viola yedoensis Makino*), simmer in water and serve.

10. LEUCORRHOEA WITH AN ODOUR. Take 60 grams of the plant and 30 grams of san bai cao roots (Chinese lizard-tail root, *Saurus chinensis (Lour.) Baill.*) plus some lean pork. Boil together into a soup, adding a little salt and sesame oil for flavour. Eat the meat and drink the soup.

11. ATROPINE POISONING. Take 250 grams of the roots of the plant, simmer in water, blend in some brown sugar and serve.

CAUTION: *If suffering a cold, empty feeling or infection of the vulva, avoid this plant.*

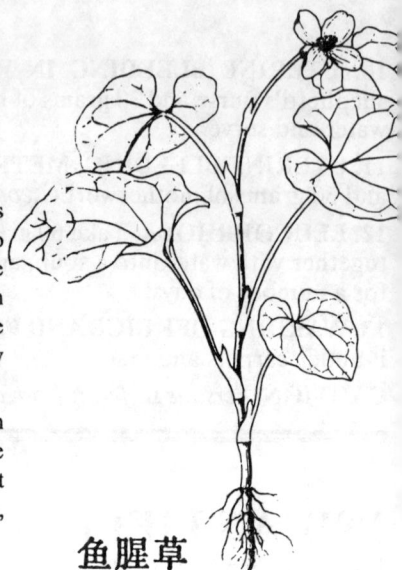

CHICKWEED
GOOSE INTESTINE VEGETABLE
Stellaria media (L.) Cyr.
E CHANG CAI

Chickweed, e chang cai (goose intestine vegetable) is also called fan lu (numerous threads), e chang cao (goose intestine grass), shen jin teng (stretch sinew vine) and yuan suan cai (garden sour vegetable). It is a perennial plant, the stem covered in fine hairs. The leaves grow in pairs and are heart shaped and thin. The flowers grow on the ends of the branches at the top of the plant or singly on the leaf axil, and are white. The seed is almost round, with a small bulge on it.

The whole plant is used in medicine. It contains saponin. The flavour is sweet-sour, its nature cool and it affects the kidneys and large intestine. It can cool a fever, neutralize poison, disperse blood stasis and ease pain.

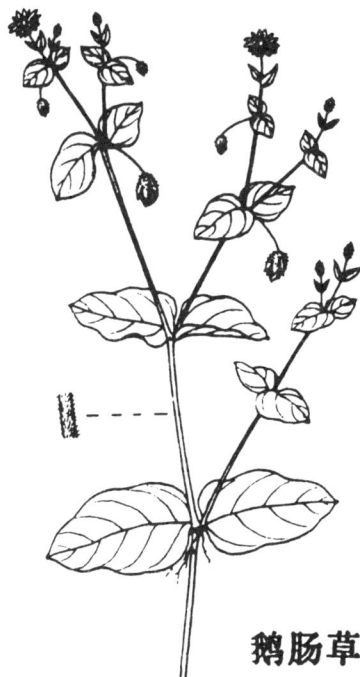

鹅肠草

APPLICATIONS
1. DYSENTERY; ENTERITIS. Take 60 grams of chickweed, simmer in water and discard the sediment, add some brown sugar and serve.

2. APPENDICITIS. Take some chickweed, crush to obtain the juice. Serve 50 mls in warm sweet wine 2-3 times a day. (Sweet wine is made from glutinous rice, sake may be used. Ed.)

3. BLOOD STASIS AND STOMACH PAINS AFTER GIVING BIRTH. Take 60 grams of chickweed, 30 grams of Chinese hawthorn and 30 grams of brown sugar. Simmer in water and drink as a tea.

4. URINARY INFECTION. Take 60 grams of chickweed, simmer in water and drink as a tea.

5. PAINFUL BRUISES AND SWELLINGS DUE TO FALLS; SWOLLEN BOILS AND CARBUNCLES. Take 60 grams of chickweed, simmer in water, mix with some wine and serve. In addition wash some chickweed, crush it, add a little salt and apply as a dressing to the affected place.

6. ULCERATED BOILS. Roast some chickweed into charcoal then grind to powder. Blend with sesame oil and apply as a dressing to the affected parts.

CAUTION: *Persons suffering with a cold empty feeling in the spleen and stomach should avoid this plant.*

CEYLON SPINACH

BASELLA
Basella rubra L.
LA KUI

(This useful vegegable has become increasingly popular in the Australian home vegetable garden in recent years and is known equally well under the name of Basella or Ceylon Spinach. Ed.)

Basella, la kui (fall behind flower) is also called yan zhi dou (rouge bean), teng cai (vine vegetable), hong teng cai (red vine vegetable), hua cai (slippery vegetable) and ruan jin cai (flexible sinew vegetable).

It is an annual vine (but can live longer), smooth and fleshy. The stem readily branches and is green or purple in colour. The leaves are egg shaped or nearly round with smooth edges. The flowers are pale violet or pink. The fruit is egg shaped or round, deep purple and juicy. (The juice stains the skin red and was once used as rouge in China. Ed.)

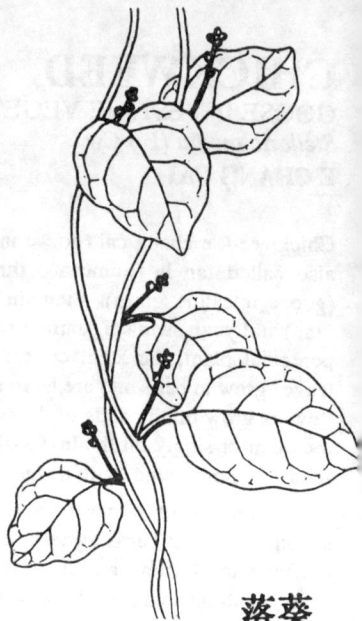

落葵

The whole plant is used in medicine. It contains glucose, mucopolysaccharide, carotene, iron, etc.

The flavour is sweet and bland, its nature cool, and it affects both great and small intestines. It can cool a fever, neutralize poison, moisten the intestines and relax the bowels.

APPLICATIONS

1. DYSENTERY. Take 100 grams of basella, simmer in water, add white or brown sugar and serve.

2. APPENDIX PAINS. Take 100 grams of basella, simmer in water, add sugar and serve frequently as a tea. In addition take some basella, wash, crush and apply to the affected place. Seek medical advice.

3. FLOW OF URINE BRIEF AND ASTRINGENT. Take 100 grams of basella, simmer in water and drink frequently as a tea.

4. BLOOD IN THE MOTIONS. Take 100 grams of basella, and a plucked and gutted hen, add water and steam till cooked. Eat frequently.

5. CONSTIPATION. Eat basella as a vegetable at every meal for a number of days.

6. BURNS AND SCALDS. Take some basella, wash clean and crush to obtain the juice. Apply this to the affected parts.

7. BOILS; SWELLING DUE TO BUMPS AND FALLS. Crush some basella and use as a dressing.

CAUTION. *Persons with a weak, empty feeling in stomach and spleen or half congealed stools should avoid this vegetable.*

STONE OIL RAPE
Pilea cavaleriei Levl. subsp. valida C.J. Chen
SHI YOU CAI

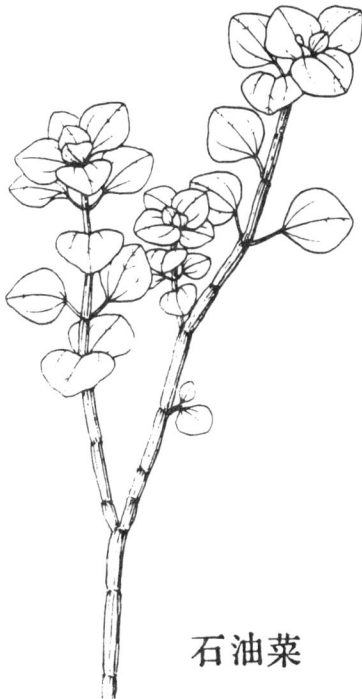

石油菜

Stone oil rape, shi you cai (stone oil vegetable) is also called shi xian cai (stone amaranth vegetable), fei nu nu cao (stone flower vegetable) and gau ji cao (malnutrition grass).

It is a fleshy plant, the stem is vertical and robust growing to a height of 250-400mm. The leaves grow on the upper part of the branches and are wide, egg shaped and with smooth edges. The stem and leaves are used in medicine. The flavour is sweet but bland, its nature cool and it affects lungs and bladder. It can cool a fever, neutralize poison, moisten the lungs, relieve coughing, diminish swelling and ease pain.

APPLICATIONS

1. TUBERCULOSIS. Take 60 grams of the plant, some pork bones and 600 mls of water. Simmer till reduced to 200 mls. Divide into 2 doses and serve in the course of a day. Continue this treatment for a fortnight then have a break of 2-3 days. After this another course can be undertaken.

2. COUGHING AND HOT FEELING IN THE LUNGS. Take 50 grams of the plant, simmer in water and later blend in sugar and serve.

3. NEPHRITIS WITH DROPSY. Take 200 grams of the plant, add water and simmer for about two hours in order to obtain 200 mls of medicinal liquid. Divide into 2 doses and serve in the course of a day. Repeat this for a number of days.

4. SWOLLEN AND PAINFUL GUMS. Take 100 grams of the plant, add some water and simmer for about 2 hours to obtain one small soup bowl of medicinal liquid. Divide into 2 doses and serve.

5. BURNS AND SCALDS. Wash the plant, crush it to obtain the juice and apply this to the affected parts.

6. SWELLING DUE TO FALLS AND INJURIES: SWOLLEN BOILS AND SORES. Crush the plant and apply to the affected place as a dressing.

CAUTION: *Persons with weak kidneys should avoid this plant.*

ASIATIC CENTELLA
Centella asiatica (L.) Urban.
LEI GONG GEN

Asiatic centella, lei gong gen (Thunder God root) is also called ji xue cao (gather snow grass) beng da wan (broken great bowl), ma ti cao (horse hoof grass) and niu rou cai (cow meat vegetable). It is a perennial creeper, thin and long. Roots grow from the nodes. The leaves also grow from the nodes and are round or shaped like a horse hoof with a long stem.

The whole plant is used in medicine. It contains vitamins B1, B2, C, carotene, tannin etc. The flavour of the plant is bitter-sweet, its nature cold and it affects the heart, stomach and bladder. It can cool a fever, neutralize poison, promote diuresis, disperse blood stasis and ease pain.

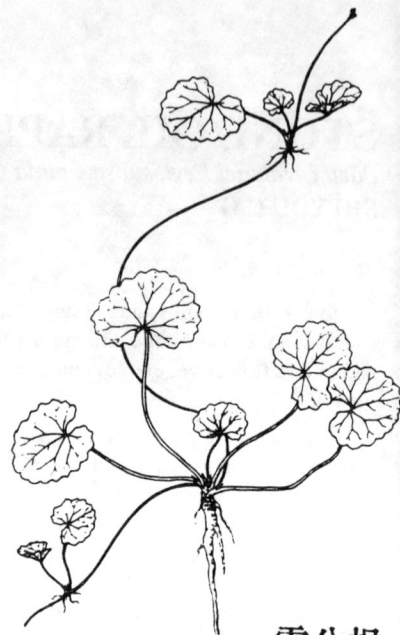

雷公根

APPLICATIONS
1. **UREMIA.** Take 500-1000 grams of the plant, crush to obtain the juice and drink this frequently.

2. **COUGHING BLOOD; VOMITING BLOOD; NOSE BLEEDING.** Take 500 grams of centella, wash clean, crush to obtain the juice and serve.

3. **WILD MUSHROOM POISONING; POISONING FROM HEART-BREAK GRASS** (*Gelsemium elegans*, this plant was once used in China as a criminal poison. Ed.).Take 500-1000 grams of centella, wash clean and crush to obtain the juice. Sip a small amount frequently.

4. **IRRITABILITY AND EXCESSIVE THIRST CAUSED BY WIND AND HEAT.** Take 60 grams of centella and 4 crushed white-necked earthworms. Simmer in water and serve.

5. **INFLAMATION OF THE THROAT.** Take some centella, wash clean and crush to obtain the juice. Add a little vinegar and sip, holding it in the mouth for as long as possible.

6. **INFECTIOUS HEPATITIS.** Take 120 grams of centella, place in 500 mls of water and simmer till it has reduced by half. Add some sugar and stir until dissolved. Divide into 2 doses and serve daily for a week. This constitutes one course of treatment.

7. **CHRONIC HEPATITIS.** Take 250 grams of centella and some chicken meat, cook together and serve.

8. **AGITATION; CHRONIC THIRST; DIARRHOEA; VOMITING.** Take some centella, wash clean and crush to obtain the juice. Blend with a little honey and serve.

9. **PLEURISY; ACHES AND PAINS IN OLD WOUNDS.** Take some centella, dry it in the sun and then crush it to powder. At regular intervals take a gram in warm boiled water.

10. **WHOOPING COUGH IN CHILDREN.** Take 30 grams of centella and some lean pork. Simmer together for an hour. Divide into 2 doses and serve in the course of a day. Repeat this for a number of days.

11. **MEASLES.** Take some centella, simmer in water and drink as a tea.

12. WHITISH, MUDDY URINE. Take 250 grams of centella, wash clean and crush to obtain the juice. Add sugar and serve.

13. SWOLLEN ANUS IN NEWLY BORN CHILD. Take some centella, simmer in water and wash the affected parts with the liquid.

CAUTION: *Persons suffering a cold, empty feeling in the spleen and stomach should avoid this plant.*

FALSE CROWNDAISY CHRYSANTHEMUM

Crassocephalum crepidioides (Benth.) S. Moore

JIA TONG HAO

The false crowndaisy chrysanthemum, jia tong hao is also called ye tong hao (wild crowndaisy chrysanthemum) and ge ming cai (revolution vegetable). It is an annual with a vertical stem. The leaves scattered along the stem vary in shape but can be long and narrow or somewhat egg shaped, with a serrated edge or somewhat fiddle-shaped. The back of the leaf is grey-green.

The flowers are small, numerous and red. The fruit is cylindrical and with vertical ribs. The whole plant is used in medicine.

It contains carotene, vitamins B1, C, etc. Its flavour is slightly bitter, its nature neither warm nor cool and it affects the spleen. It can invigorate the spleen and diminish swelling.

假茼蒿

APPLICATIONS

1. WEAKNESS IN SPLEEN AND STOMACH; DROPSY IN THE LIMBS. Take 500 grams of false crowndaisy and an equal quantity of pork or beef bones. Simmer with water into a soup and serve.

2. DROPSY CAUSED BY POOR NUTRITION. Take 500 grams of false crowndaisy, add one or two eggs, simmer with water into a soup and serve.

3. WHITE DYSENTERY (Dysentery characterized by a white mucous stool). Take 500 grams of false crowndaisy, plus some chicken meat. Simmer into a soup and serve.

DUCK FOOT VEGETABLE

Artemisia lactiflora Wall. ex DC.

YA JIAO CAI

Duck foot vegetable, ya jiao cai, is also called tian cai zi (sweet vegetable), ya jiao ai (duck foot mugwort) and si ji cai (four seasons vegetable).

It is a perennial plant with a vertical stem and few branches. The leaves growing from the main stem are wide, with deep or shallow splits and shaped somewhat like a duck's foot, hence the name.

The flowers are small and white. The whole plant is used in medicine. It contains volatile oils, yellow ketone, phenol, amino acid, coumarin, etc.

Its flavour is sweet and slightly bitter, its nature neither warm nor cool and it affects the spleen and liver.

It is good for menstrual problems, helps purify the blood, regulate the qi, moisten the internal organs, neutralize poison and diminish swelling.

鸭脚菜

APPLICATIONS

1. IRREGULAR MENSTRUATION. Take some duck foot vegetable and meat or egg and simmer into a soup. Serve at regular intervals.

2. AMENORRHOEA; STOMACH ACHE BEFORE MENSTRUATION. Take 60 grams of duck foot vegetable, simmer in water, add a little wine and brown sugar and serve.

3. BLOOD STASIS AND STOMACH PAINS AFTER GIVING BIRTH. Take 60 grams of duck foot vegetable, simmer in water, add brown sugar and serve.

4. DIZZINESS OR VERTIGO IN WOMEN. Take 100 grams of the tender shoots of the duck foot vegetable, add 2 eggs and boil into a soup. Serve this for several days.

5. LEUCORRHEA. Take 30-60 grams of duck foot vegetable, simmer in water and serve.

6. COUGH WITH BURNING FEELING IN THE LUNGS. Take 60 grams of duck foot vegetable, 6 grams of peppermint, 120 grams of bean curd and 60 grams of white sugar. Simmer in water and serve.

7. YELLOW JAUNDICE. Take 60 grams of duck foot vegetable, 30 grams of roots of the day lily and 30 grams of capillary artemisia *(Artemisia capillaris)*. Simmer in water and serve.

8. BLOOD IN THE URINE AND STOOLS. Take 30 grams each of duck foot vegetable, dried *Herba Ecliptae*, dog liver vegetable *(Dicliptera chinensis (L.)Nees)*, and Asiatic plantain. Wash clean and crush then add the water in which rice has been washed for the second time. Obtain the juice, add some sugar and serve once a day for 2-4 days.

9. BLOOD STASIS AND SWELLING DUE TO FALLS AND ACCIDENTS. Take 60 grams of duck foot vegetable and 30 grams of Chinese chives or fragrant flowered garlic *(Radix Allii Tuberosi)*. Crush together, add a little wine, stir fry till cooked and apply as a dressing to the affected parts.

RED BACK VEGETABLE
Gynura bicolor (Willd.)DC.
HONG BEI CAI

Red back vegetable, hong bei cai, is also called hong fan xian (red foreign amaranth), mu er cai (wood ear vegetable) and dang gui cai (Chinese angelica vegetable). It is a perennial plant with a vertical stem and branches on the upper part.

The leaves vary in shape from inverted egg shape to lanceolate, the reverse side is purple-red. The flowers are small, numerous and scarlet. The seed is cylindrical. The whole plant is used in medicine.

It contains yellow ketone. The flavour is sweet and slightly bitter, its nature cool and it affects the stomach and large intestine. It can cool the blood, stop bleeding, cool a fever and neutralize poison.

红背菜

APPLICATIONS

1. COUGHING BLOOD; BRONCHITIS; SUNSTROKE. Take 30-120 grams of the vegetable, simmer in water and serve.

2. AMOEBIC DYSENTERY. Take 60 grams of red back vegetable and some pickled bamboo shoot, or the liquid in which it has been pickled. Simmer in water and serve.

3. PAINFUL MENSTRUATION, DYSMENORRHOEA. Take 60 grams of red back vegetable, crush it, add a little wine, simmer in water and serve.

4. PELVIC INFECTION. Take 60 grams of red back vegetable and 30 grams of echangcai, goose intestine vegetable (*Stellaria Media L.*), simmer in watrer and serve.

5. LUMBAGO DUE TO PYELONEPHRITIS, INFLAMATION OF THE RENAL PELVIS. Take 60 grams of red back vegetable, 30 grams of duck foot vegetable (*Artemissia Lactiflora Wall. ex DC.*) and 30 grams of dog liver vegetable (*Dicliptera chinensis*). Simmer in water and serve.

MORNING GLORY
(A variety)
Merremia hederacea (Burm. f.) Hall. f.
PA LI CAI

(This plant appears to be a variety of morning glory with a small yellow flower. Ed.)

Pa li cai (climb fence vegetable), is also called mo luan teng, li lan wang (fence railing net) and guo tian wang (pass day net). It is a twining or creeping plant. The leaves have a long stalk and are heart or egg shaped, usually with three lobes. The edges often have irregular teeth. The capsule is a flattened ball shape or wide, oval and conical.

The whole plant is used in medicine. Its flavour is sweet and insipid, its nature cool and it affects the lungs and the bladder. It can cool a fever, neutralise poison, promote diuresis and disperse wetness-evil.

爬篱菜

APPLICATIONS

1. COMMON COLD; SUNSTROKE. Take 60 grams of the plant, simmer in water and drink as a tea.

2. OLIGURIA; URINE YELLOW, DEFICIENT AND ASTRINGENT. Take 60 grams of the plant, 30 grams of Asiatic centella and 30 grams of Asiatic plantain. Simmer in water and serve.

3. TONSILLITIS; LARYNGITIS. Take a quantity of the plant, wash clean and slowly chew it, holding it in the throat for a long time.

4. LEUCORRHOEA. Take 250 grams of the plant and 100 grams of beef. Add sesame oil, salt and wine and blend in for flavour. Add water and cook this into a soup and serve it for several days.

BLACK NIGHTSHADE
Solanum photeinocarpum Nakamura et Odashima
LONG KUI
(Note. Though edible this plant contains poison.)

The black nightshade, long kui (dragon plant) is also called bai hua cai (white flower vegetable) and tian tian guo (day day fruit). It is an annual with a robust vertical stem.

The leaves grow opposite each other and and are egg shaped. The inflorescence resembles a scorpion's tail and has a small cluster of white flowers.

The berry is round and about 8mm in diameter. When ripe it becomes black. The seed is egg-shaped and 1.5-2mm in diameter. The whole plant is used in medicine.

龙葵

It contains fat, steroid alkaloid, saponin, coumarin etc. The flavour is bitter-sweet, its nature cold and it contains a certain amount of poison. It affects the lungs. It can cool a fever, neutralize some poisons, clear phlegm, stop coughing, promote diuresis and reduce swelling.

APPLICATIONS

1. CHRONIC TRACHEITIS. Take 30 grams of black nightshade, 10 grams of the root of the balloonflower *(Platycodon grandifloru)* and 6 grams of licorice. Simmer in water and serve.

2. BRONCHIAL ASTHMA. Take 250 grams of complete, unbroken fruits of the black nightshade and soak in half a litre of wine for 20-30 days. Every day take a dessertspoon full, 3 times.

3. ACUTE MASTITIS. Take 30 grams of black nightshade, simmer in water, divide into 2 doses and serve in the course of a day. Repeat this for several days.

4. LARYNGOPHARYNGITIS; THROAT INFECTION. Take some leaves of black nightshade, wash clean then chew them to obtain the juice and slowly swallow it.

5. STOMACH-ACHE, HERNIA. Take 30 grams of black nightshade, simmer in water, add a little wine and serve.

6. TINEA . Take some black nightshade, simmer in water till it reduces to a thick liquid and use this to wash the affected parts.

CAUTION: *Persons suffering with a cold, empty feeling in the spleen and stomach should not eat this plant. Note also that the plant does contain some poison.*

DOG LIVER VEGETABLE
Diclleptera chinensis (L.) Nees
GOU GAN CAI

Dog liver vegetable, gou gan cai, is also called zhu gan cai (pig liver vegetable), yang gan cai (sheep liver vegetable) and lu bian ging (road side green). It is an annual or may grow for two years. The stem is vertical with many branches. The branches have swollen nodes at regular intervals and the leaves, which grow opposite each other, spring from these. The leaves are egg shaped and ovate.

The flowers are small and pink, 10-12mm long, and also grow from the branch nodes. The whole plant is used in medicine. It contains organic acid, amino acid, saccharide, etc. The flavour is sweet and insipid, its nature cool and it affects the heart and liver. It can cool fever, pacify the liver, cool the blood and neutralize poison.

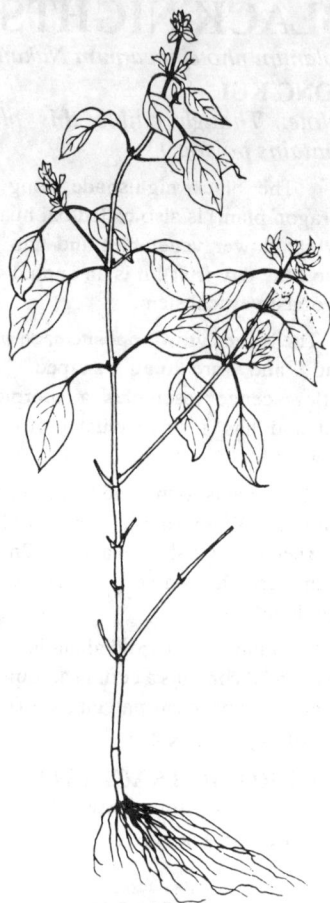

狗肝菜

APPLICATIONS

1. INFLUENZA WITH ERUPTIONS. Take 60 grams of dog liver vegetable and 60 grams of red back vegetable, simmer with 3 bowls of water until reduced to 1 bowl. Break in a green shelled duck egg, let this cook and serve.

2. COMMON COLD CAUSED BY WIND-HEAT. Take 60 grams of dog liver vegetable, simmer in water and serve.

3. INFANTILE MALNUTRITION. Take some dog liver vegetable and lean pork. Chop together, add a little salt for flavour and steam, then serve.

4. HEMATURIA, BLOOD IN THE URINE; CHYLURIA, MILKY URINE. Take 30 grams of dog liver vegetable and 30 grams of purslane, simmer in water and serve.

5. LEUCORRHOEA CAUSED BY HOT DAMP CONDITIONS. Take 100 grams of dog liver vegetable, add some lean pork, cook into a soup and serve.

6. ACUTE CONJUNCTIVITIS. Take 60 grams of dog liver vegetable and 10 grams of Chrysanthemum flowers, simmer in water and serve.

SPIT FIRE VEGETABLE
Murdannia braceata (C.B.Clarke) O.Ktze. ex J.K.Morton
TAN HUO CAI

Spit fire vegetable, tan huo cai, is also called da bao shui zhu ye (great bud water bamboo leaf), tan huo cao (phlegm fire grass), li zi cao (scrofula grass), shi zi cao (lion grass) and ai cao (cancer grass)

It is a perennial creeper with fibrous roots which grow along the stem. The leaves vary in shape but are generally narrow and pointed 150-250mm long and 10-20mm wide. The cymose inflorescence is gathered into a head. The petals are azure blue or change to purple.

The capsule contains 2 seeds. The whole plant is used in medicine. The flavour is sweet and insipid, its nature cool and if affects the liver and lungs. It can cool a fever, disperse phlegm, relieve depression and disperse tension.

痰火菜

APPLICATIONS
1. HOT COUGH WITH COPIOUS PHLEGM. Take 60 grams of the plant, cook into a soup and eat.

2. SCROFULA. Take a quantity of the plant, simmer in water, add sugar and serve.

CAUTION: *Persons suffering from a deficiency of vital energy and a cold feeling in the stomach should avoid this plant.*

PLANTAIN
RIPPLEGRASS, WAYBREAD
Plantago major L.
CHE QIAN CAO
(This is a common weed in Western gardens. Ed.)

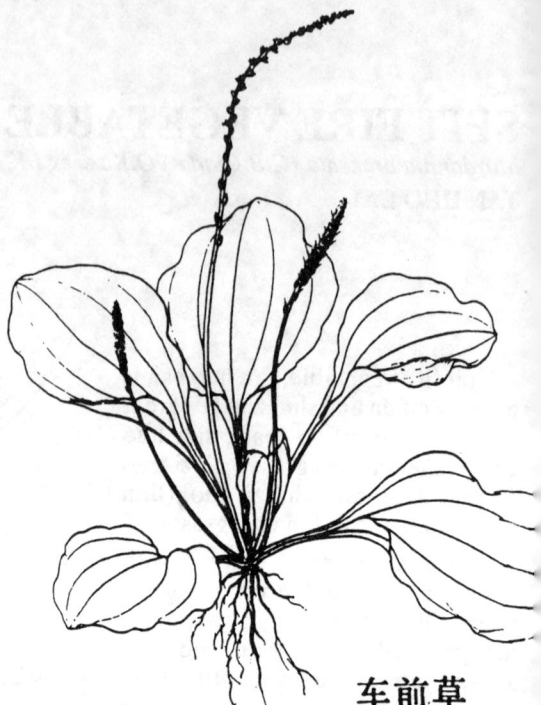

The plantain, che qian cao (wheel front grass) is also called che lun cai (wheel rotate vegetable), da che qian (great wheel front) and qian guan cao (front pierce grass). It is a perennial plant with fibrous roots. The leaves are egg shaped or broad and round with an undulating edge. The small flowers grow on a long spike. The capsule is tapered and contains 6-10 brown-black seeds.

车前草

The whole plant is used in medicine. The seed contains abundant mucilage, succinic acid, plantain sugar, choline, citric acid, vitamin C etc. The flavour of the plantain is sweet, its nature slightly cool and it affects lungs, kidney and bladder. It can cool a fever, stop bleeding, promote diuresis, aid urinary problems, dispel phlegm and ease coughing.

APPLICATIONS

1. DIFFICULTIES IN THE FLOW OF URINE; DROPSY, OEDEMA. Take 120 grams of plantain, simmer in water, add some brown sugar and drink frequently in the place of tea.

2. BLOOD IN THE URINE, HAEMATURIA. Take 30 grams each of plantain, dog liver vegetable and red back vegetable. Wash clean, add water in which rice has been washed for the second time, crush to obtain the juice and serve.

3. WATERY DIARRHOEA DUE TO MOIST HEAT; OLIGURIA, DEFICIENCY OF URINE. Take 120 grams of plantain, simmer in water and serve.

4. BURNING FEELING IN THE LUNGS WITH A COUGH. Take 60 grams of plantain and 30 grams of cordate houttuynia *(Houttuynia cordata)*, simmer in water, add some white sugar and serve.

FALSE BUCKWHEAT
Fagopyrum dibotrys (D. Don) Hara

YE QIAO MAI

False buckwheat, ye giao mai, is also called jin qiao mai (gold buckwheat), qiao mai san qi (buckwheat three screw), kai jin suo (open gold lock) and ku qiao tou (bitter buckwheat head). It is a perennial plant and not related to domesticated buckwheat.

The main root is large, robust and brown. The stem is vertical with a number of branches. The leaf is triangular, the central part heart shaped, the end and sides tapering to a point.

野荞麦

The flowers are white or pale green. The achene is triangular and brown black. The whole plant is used in medicine. It contains protein, fat, carbohydrates, calcium, phosphorous, iron, vitamin C, etc.

The flavour is sweet-sour, its nature cool and it affects the liver. It can cool a fever, nourish the liver, improve blood circulation, diminish swelling, increase appetite and promote digestion.

APPLICATIONS

1. SWOLLEN STOMACH CAUSED BY HEPATITIS; POOR APPETITE. Take 60 grams of the whole buckwheat plant, simmer in water, add sugar and drink as a tea.

2. LUMBAGO DUE TO A SPRAINED BACK. Take 60 grams of false buckwheat root, simmer in water, add a little wine and serve.

3. SWOLLEN, PAINFUL JOINTS. Take 60 grams of the whole buckwheat plant and simmer in water. Take twice a day after meals.

4. CRAMPED SINEWS AND TENDONS. Take 60 grams of buckwheat root, simmer in water, add a little wine and serve.

5. SWOLLEN, PAINFUL THROAT. Take some root of the buckwheat, crush them with vinegar and slowly swallow.

6. STAGNATION OF THE BLOOD; DYSMENORRHOEA, PAINFUL MENSTRUATION; AMMENORRHOEA, ABSENCE OF MENSTRUATION. Take 60 grams of buckwheat root, 30 grams of hawthorn fruits and 30 grams of brown sugar. Simmer in water and serve.

7. SCALDS. Take whole dried buckwheat and crush into a powder. Add a little sesame oil and apply to the affected parts.

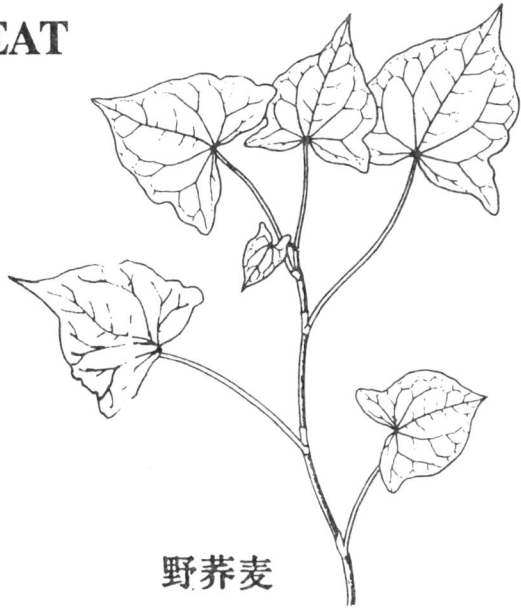

8. HAEMORRHOIDS; ANAL FISTULA. Take a quantity of the whole buckwheat plant, simmer in water and serve. In addition squat over a steaming bowl of the liquid.

9. SWOLLEN BOILS; INFECTED WOUNDS; ACUTE MASTITIS; PHLEGMON; CELLULITIS; DEEP SORES FULL OF PUS. Take a quantity of fresh buckwheat leaves, crush and apply as a dressing to the affected place. Alternatively take dried leaves, crush, add water and use these.

People seriously ill with any of the above should also take a quantity of the buckwheat plant and purslane, simmer in water and drink as a tea.

CAUTION: Persons suffering from acid stomach should avoid this plant.

MUSHROOM
Agaricus bisporus (lange) Sing.
MO GU

The mushroom, mo gu, is also called ji zu mo gu (chicken foot mushroom), mo gu xun (mushroom gill fungus) and rou xun (meat gill fungus).

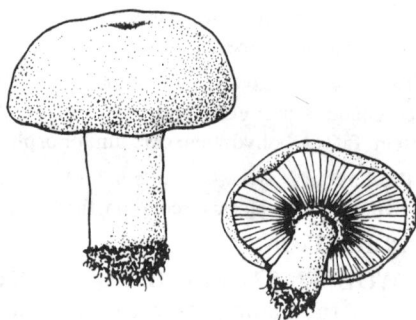

蘑菇

The upper part is like half a ball and 40-130mm in diameter. The surface is smooth, though as the mushroom ages it develops a scale-like surface. In colour it is white or grey and the stem is the same colour. The spores are purple brown and contained in the soft, flexible under-part of the dome.

The upper part of the mushroom is used in medicine. It contains protein, fat, carbohydrate, calcium, phosphorous, iron, vitamins B1, B2, C, niacin, amino acids, tyrosinase, etc.

Its flavour is sweet, its nature neither cool nor warm and it affects the liver and stomach. It can invigorate the stomach, aid digestion and benefit the liver.

APPLICATIONS

1. LACK OF APPETITE; INDIGESTION. Take some mushrooms, simmer into a soup or cook as a vegetable dish.

2. CHRONIC HEPATITIS. Take 15 grams of mushrooms and 10 grams of *Ganoderma lucidum* fungus. Simmer in water, add in sugar or salt, oil and monosodium glutamate and divide into 2-3 portions to be eaten in the course of a day. Repeat this for a fortnight, then have a 3 day break before repeating the treatment for another fortnight.

3. NUMBNESS IN HALF THE BODY, HEMIANESTHESIA. Take 15 grams of mushroom and one dace fish of about 200 grams. Boil together into a soup, add sesame oil and salt and serve once a day.

WOOD EAR
Auricularia auricula (l. ex Hook) Underw.
MU ER

(Wood ear fungus can often be bought in Eastern food shops. Westerners are warned about experimenting with wild varieties which may be unsuitable for human consumption. Ed.)

Wood ear, mu er is also known as yun er (cloud ear) and hei mu er (black wood ear).

木耳

The wood ear fungus is thin, elastic and semi-translucent. It is ear-shaped or cup-shaped, its surface smooth and red brown. It contains protein, fat, carbohydrate, calcium, phosphorous, iron, carotene, vitamins B1, B2, niacin, lecithin, cephalin, sphingomyelin, ergosterol, etc.

The flavour is sweet, its nature neither warm nor cool. It can benefit the qi, nourish blood, stop bleeding and ease pain.

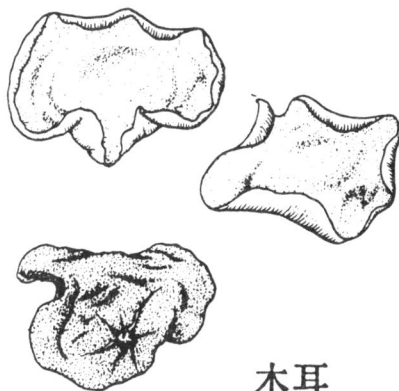

APPLICATIONS

1. DIARRHOEA DUE TO A WEAK SPLEEN. Take 10 grams of wood ear and 30 grams of sugar. Simmer in water and serve.

2. BLOOD IN THE STOOL; BLEEDING HAEMORRHOIDS; METRORRHAGIA, IRREGULAR BLEEDING FROM THE UTERUS. Take 15 grams of wood ear, add some sugar, simmer in water and serve. Repeat this for a number of days.

3. DYSENTERY WITH STOMACH PAINS. Take 15 grams of wood ear and 30 grams of brown sugar, simmer in water and serve. Repeat this for a number of days.

4. PROLAPSE OF THE RECTUM. Take 15 grams of wood ear and 30 grams of day lily, simmer together in water, add some brown sugar and serve.

5. SORES THAT TAKE A LONG TIME TO HEAL IN ELDERLY PEOPLE. Bake some wood ear then crush to a powder. Use two parts of this to one of sugar with a little water to make a paste. Apply to the affected partrs and cover with a gauze bandage. Change the dressing daily.

6. WEAKNESS AFTER CHILDBIRTH; CRAMPS AND NUMBNESS. Take 30 grams of wood ear and soak in mature vinegar for 2 hours. Divide into 2 doses and slowly chew. Another treatment is to take 15 grams of wood ear, 15 grams of brown sugar and 30 mls of honey. Mix together and steam till cooked, then divide into 3 doses and serve in the course of a day.

7. WEAKNESS DUE TO LEUCORRHOEA. Take some wood ear and roast it, then grind to a powder. Three times a day take 3 grams in warm boiled water.

8. AMENORRHOEA, ABSENCE OF MENSTRUATION. Take 30 grams of wood ear and 30 grams of su mu (*Caesalpinia sappan L.*), simmer in water. Add a little wine and serve.

9. METRORRHAGIA, IRREGULAR UTERINE BLEEDING. Take 30 grams of wood ear and stir fry till fragrant, add water and boil till cooked, add some brown sugar and serve.

LIST OF AILMENTS

ABDOMINAL PAINS see Fennel (5)

ABSCESS -infected: see Fennel (8)

ABSCESS, PULMONARY see Winter Melon (7), Yellow Soybean (8)

ACCIDENTAL SWALLOWING -of fragments of glass, metal, etc: see Chinese Chives (2)

ACHES AND PAINS -after falls and tumbles: see Chinese Chives (10)

ACHING KIDNEYS AND STOMACH -with lack of strength: see Chinese Wolfberry (3)

ACHING MUSCLES AND STIFF JOINTS see Pawpaw (6)

ACNE see Leaf-Beet Swiss Chard (5)

ACUTE BACTERIAL DYSENTARY see Chinese Bitter Vegetable (1)

ACUTE CONJUNCTIVITIS (see CONJUNCTIVITIS)

ACUTE GASTROENTERITIS see Garlic (7)

ACUTE NEPHRITIS -with Dropsy: see Bottle Gourd (1)

ACUTE THROAT INFLAMATION (see THROAT)

AGITATION see Sweet Kudzu Vine (7)

ALCOHOL, EXCESSIVE (see also HANGOVER), -to sober up: see Sweet Kudzu Vine (6)

ALCOHOLISM, CHRONIC see Yam Bean (1)

ALLERGIC DERMATITIS see Chinese Chives (15)

ALLERGIC REACTION -to paint: see Amaranth (4)

AMENORRHOEA -in pregnant women: see Sword Bean (7)

ANEMIA -prolonged caused by malaria: see Hot Pepper (5), see Spinach (3), -with Dropsy: see Black Soybean (6)

ANGINA PECTORIS see Chinese Onion (1)

ANOREXIA see Chinese Potato (1)

ANUS, CHRONIC PROLAPSE see Bamboo Shoot (3)

ANXIETY see Chinese Wolfberry (10)

APPENDIX, -inflamation of: see Chinese Bitter Vegetable (3)

APPETITE, LACK OF see Chinese Yam (5), Chinese Potato (1), Kohlrabi (1)

ARTHRITIS AND RHEUMATISM -chronic: see Eggplant (3)

ASCITES -due to cirrhosis of the liver: see Garlic (8), Bean Sprouts (4)

ASTHENIA see Cluster Mallow (4)

ASTHMA see Peanut (10), Chinese Artichoke (1), Chinese Yam (4), Chinese Kale (3), Chinese Yam (2)

ATHELETE'S FOOT see Pawpaw (5)

AVERSION TO LIGHT see Cordate Telosma (1)

BALDNESS -in the early stages: see Leaf Mustard (4), Ginger (12)

BEAUTY SPOTS -on the face: see Pea (5)

BED-WETTING -in small children: see Black Soybean (3), Carland Chrysanthemum (4)

BEE STING see Chinese Bitter Vegetable (8), Amaranth (6)

BERIBERI -leading to dropsy: see Rice Bean (2), Black Soybean (5), Peanut (6) -with Dropsy: see Yellow Soybean (2)

BILLARY ASCARIASIS see Chinese Onion (7)

BIRTH -becoming dizzy or fainting after giving birth: see Chinese Chives (8) -blood poisoning and stomach pains after giving birth: see Flowering Chinese Cabbage (4) -Heart pains and blood poisoning after giving birth: see Arrowhead (4) -vomiting clear liquid after giving birth: see Chinese Chives (9)

BITE -silver ring snake: see Eggplant (5)

BLEEDING -from the nose: see Water Spinach (3)

BLEEDING GUMS see Sweet Kudzu Vine (4), Tomato (2)

BLEEDING HAEMORRHOIDS see Chinese Chives (6)

BLEEDING, IRREGULAR IN WOMEN -not associated with menstruation: see Chinese Chives (6)

BLEEDING, NOSE see Amaranth (3), Chinese Chives (6), Radish (8), Sweet Kudzu Vine (4), Lotus Root (4)

BLEEDING -uterine: see Celery (2), Loofah (2)

BLINDNESS, NIGHT see Carrot (4), Chinese Wolfberry (4), Sweet Potato (5)

BLOATED FEELING see Cluster Mallow (1)

BLOOD, COUGHING -and lungs inflamed: see Lotus Root (7), Arrowhead (1)

BLOOD -in stools, hot: see Sweet Kudzu Vine (5),Sweet Potato (4) -in the faeces and urine: see
  Daylily (4), Water Spinach (4) -in the faeces: see Eggplant (1), Rose of Sharon (2), Water
  Dropwort (2), Chinese Chives (6) -in the urine: see Chinese Chives (6), Celtuce (4),
  Chinese Bitter Vegetable (4), Coffee Senna (4) -irregular bleeding not associated with
  menstruation: see Chinese Chives (6), -vomiting after an accident: see Flowering Chinese
  Cabbage (1), -vomiting of: see Rose of Sharon (2)

BLOOD LOSS -or poor blood: see Bean Sprouts (1)

BLOOD POISONING AND STOMACH PAINS -after giving birth: see Flowering Chinese
  Cabbage (4), -with heart pains after giving birth: see Arrowhead (4), -lack of iron leading to
  poor blood: see Spinach (3)

BLOOD PRESSURE -high: see Cucumber (4), Onion (1), Radish (7)

BLURRED VISION see Cordate Telosma (1)

BODY PAINS -and bitter taste in mouth during summer: see Bitter Melon (1)

BOILS AND CARBUNCLES -painful and swollen: see Spring Onions (6), Arrowhead (5)

BOILS AND SORES -which do not close up: see Cordate Telosma (2), Bitter Melon (7),
  Leaf-Beet Swiss Chard (4), -in the early stages: see Yellow Soybean (7) -on the back of the
  neck: see Chinese Bitter Vegetable (6), -on the fingers: see Flowering Chinese Cabbage (5),
  -infected: see Flowering Chinese Cabbage (7), Fennel (8), Garlic (11), Rose of Sharon (9),
  Water Spinach (8), Bitter Melon (8)

BREAST FEEDING -difficulty in, caused by inflamed throat in a baby: see Daylily (8)

BREAST PAIN -in woman: see Sword Bean (8)

BREASTS -swollen and painful: see Cluster Mallow (2), Spring Onions (2), -lack of breast milk:
  see Cluster Mallow (2), -swollen and painful: see -difficulty in expressing milk: see Spring
  Onions (2), -to improve flow of milk: see Wild Rice Stem (1), -with insufficient breast milk:
  Lettuce (Celtuce) (1), Loofah (1), Peanut (5), Pawpaw (1)

BREATH, BAD see Celtuce (3), Sweet Kudzu Vine (8)

BRONCHITIS -chronic: see Loofah (4), Chinese Onion (6), Peanut (9)

BURNS AND SCALDS see Chinese Potato (4), see Sword Flower (5), see Wild Rice Stem (2),
  see Yellow Soybean (5)

CARBUNCLES AND BOILS -painful and swollen: see Spring Onions (6), Arrowhead (5), Bitter
  Melon (8)

CASSAVA POISONING see Radish (10)

CATERPILLAR STINGS (see also STINGS) -that feel alternatively hot and cold: see Amaranth
  (7) CENTIPEDE STINGS (see also STINGS) see Amaranth (5), see Garlic (10), see Water
  Spinach (9)

CHEST -suffocating feeling in: see Oriental Pickling Melon (1), -tight, oppressive feeling in: see
  Coriander (2) & (4), see Sweet Kudzu Vine (7)

CHICKEN POX -in small children: see Mung Bean (2), Carrot (3)

CHILBLAINS see Hot Pepper (3), see Eggplant (8), see Lotus Root (2)

CHOKING FEELING -in the diaphragm: see Chinese Chives (3)

CHOKING -with nausea: see Broad Bean (1)

CHOLESTEROL -high levels: see Celery (1)

CHRONIC BRONCHITIS see Loofah (4), see Peanut (9)

CHRONIC CONSTIPATION (see CONSTIPATION)

CHRONIC GASTROENTERITIS (see GASTROENTERITIS)

CHRONIC PROLAPSE OF THE ANUS see Bamboo Shoot (3)

CHRONIC RHEUMATISM AND ARTHRITIS see Eggplant (3)

CHRONIC THIRST see Rose of Sharon (5), Mung Bean (3)

CHRONIC TRACHEITIS see Eggplant (4), Rose of Sharon (4)

CHYLURIA see Celery (3)

CIRRHOSIS OF THE LIVER -early stages: see Bean Sprouts (4), -with Ascites: see Bottle
  Gourd (2)

CLOUDY URINE (see URINE)

COAL GAS POISONING -with fainting: see Radish (9)

COLD, COMMON see Chinese Kale (1), -with fever and headache: see Sweet Kudzu Vine (2), -with fever during hot weather: see Bitter Melon (1), -preventative measure: see Garlic (1), Bamboo Shoot (2), Chinese Kale (1), -with chest pains: see Thorny Coriander (1), -with dry mouth and bitter taste in mouth: see Bean Curd (1), -with headache and dry heat: see Spring Onions (1), -with headache: see Leaf Mustard (1)

COLD FEELING, CONSTANT see Hot Pepper (5)

COLIC -renal: see Pawpaw (3), see Sweet Potato (2)

CONJUNCTIVITIS -acute contagious: see Bitter Melon (6), Chinese Wolfberry (2), Coffee Senna (5) CONSTANT HUNGRY FEELING -even after eating: see Mung Bean (4)

CONSTIPATION -chronic: see Coffee Senna (2), -habitual: see Spinach (2), Cluster Mallow (1), Onion (2), Radish (3), Sweet Potato (1), Sweet Potato (3)

CORNS see Garlic (12)

COUGH -associated with a cold: see Ginger (1) -with excessive frothy phlegm: see Ginger (2), caused by wind and cold: see Radish (5), -dry and hot: see Sword Flower (2), hollow; see Chinese Artichoke (1), Pumpkin (1), -hot, with coughing up blood: see Broad Bean (8), -hot,with excessive phlegm: see Chinese Cabbage (1), Thorny Coriander (1), -with dry mouth, difficulty in coughing up phlegm: see Bean Curd (2)

COUGH, ASTHMATIC -with excessive phlegm: see Chinese Yam (4), see Peanut (10), Chinese Kale (3)

COUGHING AT NIGHT see Dill (1)

COUGHING BLOOD see Arrowhead (1)

COUGHING -with excessive phlegm: see Carland Chrysanthemum (1), -with hot phlegm: see Coffee Senna (3)

COUGH, SEARING -with copious phlegm: see Bamboo Shoot (1)

COUGH, WHOOPING -in small children: see Carrot (1), see Eggplant (2), Garlic (4), Radish (4)

CRAMPS -in hands and feet: see Yellow Soybean (3)

DERMATITIS -from paint: see Chinese Cabbage (2), Leaf Mustard (6), -allergic: see Chinese Chives (15), -nervous: see Chinese Chives (14)

DERMATITIS, PADDY FIELD see Chinese Bitter Vegetable (7)

DIABETES see Chinese Wolfberry (1), Chinese Yam (6), Tomato (1), Winter Melon (2), -with Polydipsia: see Spinach (1)

DIARRHOEA AND VOMITING see Leaf Mustard (5), see Sweet Potato (2)

DIARRHOEA -indigestion with: see Chinese Chives (7), -scalding diarrhoea in small children: see Cucumber (3), -watery, caused by disorder of the spleen: see Yellow Soybean (4), -watery: see Broad Bean (10)

DIFFICULTY IN PASSING MOTIONS see Cluster Mallow (1)

DIFFICULTY IN SWALLOWING see Coriander (8), see Sword Bean (5)

DIFFICULTY IN URINATING see Oriental Pickling Melon (3)

DIPHTHERIA -to prevent: see Chinese Kale (4)

DIZZINESS -after drinking alcohol: see Oriental Pickling Melon (1), -after giving birth: see Chinese Chives (8), -with a tight feeling around the heart: see Fennel (7)

DROPSY -caused by poor nutrition: see Cowpea (3), see Broad Bean (3),Cluster Mallow (4), Daylily (9), Winter Melon (1)

DRUNKENNESS see Broad Bean (5)

DRY HOT COUGH (see COUGH)

DRY HOT FEELING -with excessive phlegm: see Leaf Mustard (8)

DRY RETCHING see Sweet Potato (3)

DUODENAL ULCER see Cabbage (1), Kohlrabi (1), Pawpaw (2), Sword Flower (3)

DYSENTARY -acute bacterial: see Chinese Bitter Vegetable (1), -in small children: see Cucumber (1), -prevention of: see Garlic (5) Garlic (6), see Amaranth (2), Bitter Melon (5), Coffee Senna (5), Daylily (2), Leaf-Beet Swiss Chard (2), Lotus Root (1), Radish (6), Rose of Sharon (1), -with bleeding and stomach pain: see Flowering Chinese Cabbage (2)

EAR -insects in: see Celtuce (5)

ENURESIS see Black Soybean (3)

EPISTAXIS see Chinese Chives (6), Garlic (9), Amaranth (3)

ERYSIPELAS -in small children: see Mung Bean (7), Yellow Soybean (6)

EXCESSIVE FROTHY PHLEGM see Ginger (1)
EXHAUSTION AND LACK OF STRENGTH see Chinese Yam (2)
EYE -small fibres in the eye: see Chinese Cabbage (3) -red: see Cordate Telosma (1) -aversion to light: see Cordate Telosma (1) -blurred vision: see Cordate Telosma (1)

FAINTING OR DIZZINESS -after giving birth: see Chinese Chives (8)
FALLS (see INJURIES)
FAVUS -of the scalp: see Coriander (6)
FEELING OF NUMBNESS IN THE LIMBS see Rice Bean (2)
FEELING OF WEAKNESS see Chinese Chinves (1)
FEET -splits caused by extreme cold: see Lotus
Root (2)
FEVER AND THIRST see Oriental Pickling Melon (2)
FEVER -high, see Leaf-Beet Swiss Chard (1), -in small children, with palpitations of the heart with thirst: see Chinese Wolfberry (11), -with restlessness and thirst: see Sweet Kudzu Vine (1), -with vomiting in small children: see Sweet Kudzu Vine (3)
FISHBONE STUCK IN THROAT see Chinese Olive (2)
FISH SCALE MOLE see Bean Sprouts (3)
FOOD POISONING -from fish: see Winter Melon (8)
FROST-BITE see Spring Onions (5), -that has not begun to fester: see Hot Pepper (3)
FURUNCLE see Bitter Melon (7), Garlic (11)

GALL STONES see Pawpaw (3)
GAS POISONING -with fainting: see Radish (9)
GASTRIC DISORDER CAUSING NAUSEA see Leaf Mustard (3)
GASTRIC DISORDERS -with nausea: see Coriander (8), -with nausea, vomiting: see Rose of Sharon (3)
GASTRIC ULCER see Tomato (4)
GASTROENTERITIS -acute: see Garlic (7), -chronic: see Coffee Senna (2), see Chinese Onion (8)
GINGIVITIS see Tomato (2)
GLUTAMATIC PYRUVIC TRANSAMINASE -to decrease: see Peanut (1)
GUMS, BLEEDING see Sweet Kudzu Vine (4), Tomato (2)

HAEMORRHAGE, INTERNAL see Broad Bean (6)
HAEMORRHOIDS, -sore and bleeding: see Leaf-Beet Swiss Chard (3), -swollen and painful: see Leaf Mustard (7), Rose of Sharon (7), Water Spinach (5) HAIR -lacking life or lustre: see Leaf Mustard (4) -early stages of baldness: see Leaf Mustard (4), -sore and swollen: see Chinese Wolfberry (9)
HANGOVER (see also ALCOHOL) see Sweet Kudzu Vine (7)
HEADACHE -stubborn: see Coffee Senna (1), -with pus flowing from the ear: see Water Spinach (2)
HEART -coronary heart disease: see Chinese Onion (1)
HEART PAINS -and blood poisoning after giving birth: see Arrowhead (4)
HEATSTROKE see Bitter Melon (2), Mung Bean (1), -with vomiting and diarrhoea: see Pea (3)
HEAT, WORKING IN -in hot conditions or near a fire: see Celtuce (2)
HEPATITIS see Chinese Bitter Vegetable (5), see Watershield (2)
HERNIA, INCARCERATED (see INCARCERATED HERNIA)
HERNIA -in small children: see Sword Bean (4), -of the testicles: see Dill (3)
HERNIA PAIN see Coriander (4)
HERNIA SWELLING see Carland Chrysanthemum (2)
HICCUPS see Ginger (7), see Radish (2), see Sword Bean (6)
HIGH BLOOD FAT see Peanut (7)
HIGH BLOOD PRESSURE see Broad Bean (7), Celery (1), Coffee Senna (2), Cucumber (4), Daylily (1), Onion (1), Peanut (2), Radish (7)
HIGH CHOLESTEROL LEVELS see Celery (1)
HOLLOW COUGH see Pumpkin (1)
HOT, FLUSHED FEELING -with thirst: see Bitter Melon (3)

HOT FLUSHES -in a woman: see Celery (2)
HYPERLIPAEMIA see Peanut (7)

IMPETIGO see Cucumber (5)
IMPOTENCE see Chinese Chives (5)
INADEQUATE FLOW OF URINE (see URINE)
INCARCERATED HERNIA -of the small intestine: see Fennel (1)
INDIGESTION see Chinese Yam (5), Coriander (3), Kohlrabi (1), Thorny Coriander (2), -with
    diarrhoea: see Chinese Chives (7)
INFANT HOT AND UPSET see Black Soybean (4)
INFECTED BOILS see Flowering Chinese Cabbage (7)
INFLAMATION -acute, of the throat: see Chinese Bitter Vegetable (2) -of the appendix: see
    Chinese Bitter Vegetable (3), -of the breasts: see Coffee Senna (7), -of the intestines: see
    Leaf-Beet Swiss Chard (2) -of the liver: see Chinese Bitter Vegetable (5) -of the nose and
    sinus: see Chinese Wolfberry (5)
INFLAMATION OF THE KIDNEYS -with Dropsy: see Winter Melon (3)
INFLAMED BREAST AND STOMACH -with liquid in the lungs: see Winter Melon (7)
INFLAMED SORES see Sweet Potato (7)
INFLAMED THROAT IN A BABY -causing difficuly in breast feeding: see Daylily (8)
INJURIES -from falls or sprains: see Ginger (14) -pain from falls, sprains or wounds: see Sand
    Ginger (1)
INSECT BITE -centipede: see Garlic (10)
INSECT STINGS see Arrowhead (6), Chinese Onion (11), Cluster Mallow (5)
INSOMNIA see Cabbage (3), Peanut (3)
INSUFFICIENT BREAST MILK see Celtuce (Asparagus or Lettuce) (1), Pawpaw (1)
INTERNAL BLEEDING see Peanut (8)
INTERNAL STRAINS see Chinese Wolfberry (3)
INTESTINAL OBSTRUCTION see Flowering Chinese Cabbage (3)
INTESTINES, DRY see Sweet Potato (1)
INTESTINES, INFLAMATION OF THE see Leaf-Beet Swiss Chard (2)
INTOXICATION see Broad Bean (5)
ISCHURIA see Spring Onions (3)

JAUNDICE, -see Chinese Bitter Vegetable (5), -with liver inflamation: see Watershield (2),
    Amaranth (1) -affecting the colour of the whole body: see Daylily (3) Water Dropwort (3),
    Arrowhead (3)
JOINTS, -stiff, see Pawpaw (6), -unable to straighten: see Cabbage (2)

KIDNEY AND WAIST PAINS see Chinese Artichoke (2), see Black Soybean (1)
KIDNEY ASTHENIA -due to diabetes: see Black Soybean (8)
KIDNEYS AND STOMACH (see ACHING KIDNEYS AND STOMACH)
KIDNEYS -empty feeling in kidneys with dizziness and headaches: see Dill (5), -inflamation of
    with Dropsy: see Winter Melon (3)
KIDNEY STONES see Pawpaw (3)

LACK OF BREASTMILK -just before and after birth: see Pea (4)
LACK OF ENERGY see Pea (2)
LACK OF STRENGTH see Chinese Yam (1), Rice Bean (2), -with Dropsy: see Cluster Mallow
    (4)
LEAD POISONING -preventing and treating: see Garlic (13), Mung Bean (8)
LEG ULCERS see Broad Bean (11)
LEUCORRHOEA see Chinese Wolfberry (8), Coffee Senna (5), see Rose of Sharon (6), see
    Winter Melon (6)
LIVER INFLAMATION see Chinese Bitter Vegetable (5)
LOSS OF APPETITE see Chinese Potato (1), see Coriander (3), see Kohlrabi (1), see Thorny
    Coriander (2)

LUMBAGO -due to weak kidneys: see Fennel (4), -during pregnancy: see Black Soybean (10), Sword Bean (2), -with kidney pains: see Sword Bean (1) -and rheumatism: see Sword Bean (3), Loofah (3)

LUNG INFECTIONS see Leaf Mustard (2)

LUNGS, -burning feeling in with frequent coughing: see Watercress (2), -inflamed and coughing blood: see Lotus Root (7), -with burning feeling and coughing of blood: see Radish (8), -with hot feeling and a cough: see Sweet Potato (8)

MALNUTRITION -in small children due to digestive problems: see Cowpea (2), -with Dropsy: see Yellow Soybean (1)

MASTITIS see Flowering Chinese Cabbage (6), see Sweet Potato (6)

MEASLES -after recovery the child has no appetite and suffers from dysentery: see Chinese Olive (1), -inadequate eruption: see Chinese Onion (9) and Coriander (1), precaution against: see Yellow Soybean (9), Carrot (2), -with Enteritis in small children: see Mung Bean (6)

MENINGITIS, MENINGOCOCCAL -preventative measure against epidemic: see Garlic (2)

MENINGOCOCCAL MENINGITIS -see Garlic (2)

MENORRHAGIA see Hot Pepper (4)

MENSTRUATION -ahead of time: see Daylily (7), -pain in stomach or lower abdomen during: see Ginger (8)

METROPTOSIS see Pumpkin (5)

METRORRHAGIA see Black Soybean (9), see Chinese Chives (6)

MIGRAINE see Chinese Wolfberry (7), see Ginger (10), see Loofah (5)

MILK FLOW -to improve: see Wild Rice Stem (1)

MILKY URINE see Celery (3)

MOLE -fish-scale: see Bean Sprouts (3)

MOUTH -sores in the corner of: see Oriental Pickling (4) -bitter taste and body pains during summer: see Bitter Melon (1) - sores, see Coffee Senna (6)

MOUTH ULCERS see Tomato (3)

MOUTH -with a dry bitter taste in: see Leaf Mustard (1)

MUMPS see Chinese Potato (3), see Mung Bean (5), see Sword Flower (4), see Water Dropwort (5)

MUSCLES, ACHING see Pawpaw (6)

MUSCLE STRAIN -causing lumbago: see Dill (4)

NAUSEA AND VOMITING -during pregnancy: see Pawpaw (4)

NAUSEA -from gastric disorder: see Leaf Mustard (3)

NEPHRITIS -acute with Dropsy: see Bottle Gourd (1), Winter Melon (3)

NERVOUS DERMATITIS see Chinese Chives (14)

NETTLE RASH see Chinese Chives (13), see Winter Melon (5)

NIGHT BLINDNESS (see BLINDNESS)

NIGHT BLINDNESS see Carrot (4), Sweet Potato (5)

NOSE BLEEDING see Amaranth (3), Chinese Chives (6), Garlic (9), Sweet Kudzu Vine (4), Water Spinach (3), -will not stop: see Lotus Root (4)

NOSE DISCHARGE, YELLOW see Lotus Root (3)

OEDEMA see Broad Bean (3), Cluster Mallow (4), Daylily (9), Winter Melon (1)

OLIGURIA see Winter Melon (4)

OTORRHOEA see Water Spinach (2)

PAIN -caused by wind and moisture: see Spring Onions (4) -caused by falls and similar accidents: see Spring Onions (4)

PAIN, COLD -in the waist and knee: see Chinese Chives (5)

PAINS AND ACHES -after falls and tumbles: see Chinese Chives (10)

PAIN WHEN URINATING see Arrowhead (2)

PAIN WHEN URINATING (see URINE)

PALPITATIONS -of the heart: see Chinese Yam (2) -nervous, of hand, foot and heart with feverish feeling: see Chinese Yam (2)

PALPITATIONS OF THE HEART -with thirst: see Chinese Wolfberry (10) -with thirst and hectic fever in small children: see Chinese Wolfberry (11)

PEMPHIGUS see Broad Bean (12)

PEPTIC ULCER see Pawpaw (2), Sword Flower (3)

PERTUSSIS -small children: see Carrot (1)

PHLEGM, WHITE FROTHY -excessive: see Dill (1)

POISONED SORES see Sweet Potato (7)

POISONING -by Chinese Monkhead: see Mung Bean (8) -lead: see Mung Bean (8), Garlic (13), -from cassava: see Radish (10), -from eating fish: see Winter Melon (8), -from eating Pinellia Ternata: see Ginger (9), -from eating Arum Tryphyllum (jack-in-the-pulpit): see Ginger (9), -from Gelsemium Elegans: see Water Spinach (1), -of the blood and stomach pains after giving birth: see Flowering Chinese Cabbage (4), -through inhalation of petrol: see Chinese Cabbage (4)

POLYDIPSIA see Chinese Chives (4)

POOR NUTRITION -associated with dropsy: see Peanut (3), -leading to dropsy: see Rice Bean (1)

PREGNANCY -movement of foetus accompanied by stomach pain: see Chinese Onion (5), -nausea and vomiting during: see Pawpaw (4)

PROLAPSE OF THE ANUS see Coriander (5), see Daylily (5)

PROLAPSE OF THE UTERUS see Pumpkin (5)

PRURITUS see Watercress (3)

PUFFINESS OF THE FLESH see Broad Bean (2)

PULMONARY ABSCESS see Winter Melon (7), Yellow Soybean (8)

PULMONARY TUBERCULOSIS see Bean Sprouts (2), Sword Flower (1)

PULMONARY TUBERCULOSIS see TUBERCULOSIS

PUPURA see Peanut (8)

RASH -nettle: see Winter Melon (5)

RECTUM, PROLAPSE OF (see PROLAPSE)

RED EYES see Cordate Telosma (1)

REGURGITATION -with stomach pains: see Chinese Potato (2), Coriander (8)

RENAL COLIC see Pawpaw (3)

RHEUMATIC PAINS -in the joints: see Fennel (9)

RHEUMATISM AND ARTHRITIS -chronic: see Eggplant (3)

RHEUMATISM AND LUMBAGO see Sword Bean (3)

ROUNDWORM -causing intestinal obstruction: see Peanut (11), Ginger (6), Pumpkin (2), Chinese Onion (7)

RUN-DOWN FEELING see Sweet Kudzu Vine (8), Chinese Yam (1)

SCABIES see Chinese Onion (10), see Yam Bean (2)

SCALDING DIARRHOEA (see DIARRHOEA)

SCALDS AND BURNS (see BURNS AND SCALDS) see Chinese Potato (4), Sword Flower (5), Wild Rice Stem (2), Yellow Soybean (5)

SCALDS see Broad Bean (12), Pumpkin (6)

SCARS -on the head on which hair will not grow: see Celtuce (7)

SCHISTOSOMIASIS see Pumpkin (4)

SCLERODERMA -in babies: see Chinese Chives (16)

SCORPIAN BITE (see also STINGS) see Cluster Mallow (5)

SEMINAL EMISSION see Chinese Chives (5), -white and thick: see Chinese Yam (2)

SILVER RING SNAKE BITE see Eggplant (5)

SINUSITIS see Chinese Onion (4), Chinese Wolfberry (5), Lotus Root (3)

SKIN IRRITATION see Watercress (3)

SKIN MOISTURIZER see Leaf-Beet Swiss Chard (5)

SKIN -peeling off of hands: see Ginger (11) -with red or white patches: see Ginger (13), -puffiness: see Broad Bean (2) -swollen and poisoned: see Tomato (5)

SLEEP, RESTLESS -with too many dreams: see Cabbage (3)

SOBERING UP -after excessive alcohol: see Sweet Kudzu Vine (6)

SORES AND BOILS -which do not close up: see Cordate Telosma (2)

SORES -hot and painful infected, swollen: see Eggplant (6), -infected and inflamed: see Coffee Senna (8) -in the mouth: see Coffee Senna (6), -in the corner of the mouth: see Oriental Pickling (4), -that become inflamed or poisoned: see Sweet Potato (7), -with itching: see Chinese Onion (10)

SORE THROAT see Chinese Kale (2)

SPEECH -hoarse: see Daylily (6) SPERMATORRHOEA see Chinese Chives (5)

SPITTING PHLEGM WITH BLOOD see Peanut (10)

SPLEEN -with empty cold feeling: see Chinese Potato (1)

SPLINTERS IN FLESH see Sand Ginger (2)

SPRAINS (see INJURIES)

STIFF JOINTS see Cabbage (2)

STING, -bee: see Chinese Bitter Vegetable (8) Amaranth (6) -caterpillar: see Amaranth (7) -centipede: see Amaranth (5) Water Spinach (9)

STINGS, INSECT see Arrowhead (6), see Chinese Onion (11), see Cluster Mallow (5)

STOMACH ACHE see Bitter Melon (4), see Sweet Potato (2), -with a cold feeling in stomach: see Fennel (6), Coriander (7) and Hot Pepper (1), -with a cold feeling in the stomach, pale lips, vomiting with excessive saliva: see Ginger (4) -with cold feeling in the stomach, sour regurgitation, acid vomit: see Ginger (5), -with cold feeling in stomach in small children: see Dill (2), -with vomiting and diarrhoea: see Ginger (3)

STOMACH INFLAMATION see Coffee Senna (5)

STOMACH NEUROSIS see Chinese Onion (2)

STOMACH OR INTESTINAL INFLAMATION -with dry vomiting: see Chinese Onion (8)

STOMACH PAIN -in pregnancy with foetus movement: see Chinese Onion (5), and blood poisoning after giving birth: see Flowering Chinese Cabbage (4), -caused by extremely hot weather: see Wild Rice Stem (3), -hot with acid regurgitation: see Chinese Potato (2)

STOMACH -swollen and painful: see Sword Bean (7), see Sweet Potato (3), -swollen, caused by loss of vital energy: see Hot Pepper (1), -with empty cold feeling: see Chinese Potato (1)

STOMACH ULCER see Kohlrabi (1), see Pawpaw (2), see Sword Flower (3), see Cabbage (1)

STOOLS, HOT & SHOWING BLOOD see Sweet Kudzu Vine (5)

SUFFOCATING FEELING -in the chest: see Oriental Pickling Melon (1)

SUNSTROKE see Bitter Melon (2)

SWEATING -at night: see Chinese Chives (1), -excessive: see Chinese Yam (2)

SWELLING AT THE BACK OF THE NECK see Chinese Yam (7)

SWELLING IN THE LOWER ABDOMEN OF WOMAN -painful: see Dill (3)

SWELLINGS -after falls and similar accidents: see Chinese Chives (11), -innominate toxic: see Garlic (11), from falls and accidents: see Sword Flower (4), -painful: see Thorny Coriander (3)

TAPEWORM see Pumpkin (3)

TESTICLES -hernia of the: see Dill (3), -liquid accumulating under skin: see Fennel (2) -swelling: see Fennel (2) and Fennel (3), -pain in the: see Carland Chrysanthemum (2), -swollen and painful: see Celtuce (6)

THIRST AND FEVER see Oriental Pickling Melon (2)

THIRST -associated with Dropsy: see Winter Melon (4), (-often related to diabetes): see Watershield (1), -chronic: see Mung Bean (3) Rose of Sharon (5) and Spinach (1), see Sweet Kudzu Vine (7), -to diminish: see Fennel (5) and Pea (1)

THIRSTY -even after drinking: see Chinese Chives (4)

THROAT -acute inflamation: see Cucumber (2) and Chinese Bitter Vegetable (2), see Lotus Root (6), see Chinese Kale (2), -fishbone stuck in: see Chinese Olive (2)

TIGHT FEELING IN THE CHEST see Sweet Kudzu Vine (7)

TINEA see Chinese Chives (12),see Pawpaw (5)

TINEA CAPITUS -in children: see Coriander (6)

TINEA CIRCINATA -on the head: see Rose of Sharon (8)

TINEA VERSICOLOR see Eggplant (7)

TIREDNESS -run-down feeling: see Sweet Kudzu Vine (8)

TONIC -to build up strength: see Chinese Artichoke (5)

TONSILLITIS see Cucumber (2)

TOOTHACHE see Bean Curd (3), see Chinese Wolfberry (6), see Water Dropwort (4), see Water Spinach (6)

TRACHEITIS -chronic: see Chinese Onion (6), see Eggplant (4), see Rose of Sharon (4)

TRICHOMONIASIS, VAGINAL see Onion (5)

TUBERCULOSIS -of the Lymph Gland: see Chinese Artichoke (4), -pulmonary: see Bean Sprouts (2), Sword Flower (1), -with coughing blood: see Chinese Artichoke (3), Arrowhead (2) and Broad Bean (4), see Garlic (3), see Watercress (1), -with sweating at night: see Chinese Chives (1)

ULCER -duodenal: see Pawpaw (2), Sword Flower (3), Kohlrabi (1) and Cabbage (1), -stomach: see Pawpaw (2), Sword Flower (3), Kohlrabi (1) and Cabbage (1), -peptic: see Pawpaw (2), Sword Flower (3) ,-gastric: see Tomato (4), -on breasts of nursing mothers: see Sweet Potato (6), -in the mouth: see Tomato (3), -of the skin: see Onion (4),-on legs; that will not heal: see Broad Bean (11)

UNDER-ARM ODOUR see Hot Pepper (2)

URINARY PASSAGE, INFLAMED see Coffee Senna (5)

URINATING -with astringent pain: see Arrowhead (2), Water Dropwort (1) and Watercress (4), -difficulty in passing urine: see Celtuce (4), -blood in the urine: see Celtuce (4), -frequency throughout the night: see Carland Chrysanthemum (3), -frequent: see Watercress (4), -cloudy: see Watercress (4) and Celery (3), -blockage: see Broad Bean (9), -cloudy urine in males: see Winter Melon (6), -difficulty in passing of urine by small children: see Black Soybean (7), -difficulty in passing: see Spring Onions (3), Oriental Pickling (3), -flow poor or too frequent in aged people: see Chinese Yam (3), -inadequate flow of: see Winter Melon (4), -muddy: see Water Spinach (4) -difficulty in passing urine after walking long distances on hot days: see Water Spinach (7), -not making sufficient urine: see Cowpea (1)

URTICARIA see Chinese Chives (13), see Winter Melon (5)

UTERINE BLEEDING see Celery (2), see Loofah (2)

UTERUS -prolapse of: see Pumpkin (5)

VAGINAL TRICHOMONIASIS see Onion (5) VISION, FAILING see Chinese Wolfberry (4)

VITILIGO, RED OR WHITE see Ginger (13)

VOMITING AND DIARRHOEA see Leaf Mustard (5), see Sweet Potato (2)

VOMITING BLOOD -after an accident: see Flowering Chinese Cabbage (1), see Rose of Sharon (2), Sweet Kudzu Vine (4), Sweet Potato (4), -suddenly: see Lotus Root (5)

VOMITING -clear liquid: see Fennel (7), -clear liquid after giving birth: see Chinese Chives (9), -dry with stomach or intestinal inflamation: see Chinese Onion (8), Broad Bean (1) -after eating: see Sword Bean (5), Sweet Kudzu Vine (7), -with fever in small children: see Sweet Kudzu Vine (3), -with hot feeling in the stomach: see Radish (1)

WAIST AND KIDNEY PAIN see Chinese Artichoke (2)

WART -common:see Bean Sprouts (3)

WHOOPING COUGH see Eggplant (2), see Garlic (4), see Radish (4), -small children: see Carrot (1)

WOMB, WEAK AND SHRUNKEN -with difficulty in having children: see Cluster Mallow (3)

WORMS -roundworms: see Chinese Onion (7), see Pumpkin (2), -causing obsturction: see Peanut (11), -tapeworms: see Pumpkin (3)

WOUNDS (see INJURIES), see Onion (3)

YELLOW JAUNDICE (see JAUNDICE) see Arrowhead (3)

YIN DEFICIENCY -in small children, resulting in fever: see Black Soybean (2)

LATIN INDEX

INDEX OF ENGLISH NAMES